TEACH SURVIVE, REPEAT:

AN EXPOSÈ ON THE REAL CLASSROOM

Copyright © 2025 Mark Rickard

All rights reserved.

The moral rights of the author have been asserted.

No part of this publication may be reproduced, stored, or transmitted in any form or by any means—electronic, mechanical, photocopying, recording, or otherwise—without the prior written permission of the author, except for brief quotations used in reviews, academic work, or as permitted by applicable copyright law.

This book is a personal reflection based on the author's lived experiences in the teaching profession, as well as anonymised accounts shared by others with their consent. While inspired by real events and conversations, names, educational establishments, locations, and identifying details have been changed or omitted to protect privacy. Events are recalled from memory and may contain minor inaccuracies or unintentional misquotations.

Table of Contents

FOREWORD 1

PART 1.
THE TEACHING JOURNEY – EXPECTATION VS REALITY 3
    CHAPTER 1 THE ULTIMATE SURVIVAL TEST 4
    CHAPTER 2 TEACHING IN HELL'S POSTCODE 11
    CHAPTER 3 THE COST OF CARING 18

PART 2.
SYSTEMIC FAILURES – A BROKEN SYSTEM 23
    CHAPTER 4 EDUCATION INC.: THE CORPORATE TAKEOVER 24
    CHAPTER 5 PASS AT ANY COST 30
    CHAPTER 6 THE DESTRUCTIVE OFSTED MACHINE 35
    CHAPTER 7 UNQUALIFIED TAKEOVER 42
    CHAPTER 8 THE PARENT TRAP 46
    CHAPTER 9 THE IN-CROWD: POWER, PRIVILEGE AND THE COST OF BIAS 51

PART 3.
PERSONAL IMPACT – THE HUMAN COST 57
    CHAPTER 10 COLLATERAL DAMAGE OF TEACHING 58
    CHAPTER 11 SHATTERED TRUST: A TEACHER'S ORDEAL 65
    CHAPTER 12 THE MENTAL HEALTH TOLL OF TEACHING 76
    CHAPTER 13 THE SALARY SQUEEZE 84

PART 4.
TOXIC WORK ENVIRONMENTS – CULTURE AND LEADERSHIP 91
- CHAPTER 14 WHEN LEADERSHIP FAILS 92
- CHAPTER 15 NO EXCUSES, NO ESCAPE 97
- CHAPTER 16 CONFRONTING SEXUAL HARASSMENT 101
- CHAPTER 17 THE HIDDEN BULLY 107
- CHAPTER 18 AVOIDING WORK ROMANCE 113
- CHAPTER 19 SUPPLY TEACHING – A THANKLESS ART 118

PART 5.
SURVIVAL STRATEGIES – NAVIGATING THE PROFESSION 125
- CHAPTER 20 HR – THE SMILING ASSASSIN 126
- CHAPTER 21 THE EDUCATOR'S SURVIVAL TOOLKIT 131

PART 6.
A REFLECTION ON TEACHING – CHALLENGES AND HOPE 143
- CHAPTER 22 TEACHING WITHOUT BORDERS 144
- CHAPTER 23 THE GREAT ESCAPE 152
- CHAPTER 24 THE UNSUNG HEROES OF EDUCATION 159
- CHAPTER 25 MY FINAL WORD 165

SPECIAL THANKS 168

REFERENCES 169

FOREWORD

Welcome to this unapologetic exposé on the teaching profession – a job cloaked in clichés about inspiring young minds, but far removed from the idealistic image of dynamic classrooms that most envision. If you're looking for heartwarming anecdotes of transforming young lives or feel-good narratives of triumph in the face of adversity, you won't find them here. Although these moments do still exist, they are rare and have sadly been overshadowed by the harrowing actuality of modern-day teaching. What you are about to read is not some utopian dream of teaching; it's a raw, unvarnished exploration of the broken education system in UK schools today. It's the reality of the caffeine-fuelled daily grind, filled with chaos, despair and a sizeable amount of resilience.

This book doesn't name names; instead, it points fingers at a system that hundreds of thousands of teachers have invested their careers and sanity in, only to be chewed up and spat out by it. While some may cling to the illusion that the system works, countless others know it doesn't. Yet even for those who see the cracks, escaping isn't easy. Many dream of leaving, only to find themselves paralysed by fear of the unknown, the financial insecurity and the weight of starting over. Specific details and anecdotal evidence have been anonymised, partly to protect the people who have shared their experiences, but mostly to illustrate the point that these scenarios aren't isolated. They're systemic. What you'll find here is a profession crippled by an obsessive fixation with data, staffrooms rife with politics, incompetence, bullying, allegations, sexual harassment and classrooms pushed to the brink of collapse.

TEACH, SURVIVE, REPEAT

Expect staffroom truths, unflinching accounts of misbehaviour that would rattle even the most seasoned teacher, and a blistering critique of schools operating more like businesses than places of learning. Expect a no-holds-barred dive into the jargon-riddled circus of modern education: Senior Leadership Team (SLT) "learning walks" that serve more as performative surveillance than meaningful support; behaviour sanctions that collapse under the weight of endless excuses and the soul-destroying chase to tick meaningless boxes before Ofsted descends like vultures on a carcass.

This isn't a guide or a self-help manual. It's a mirror for many teachers to see their frustrations reflected and a reality check for anyone still seduced by glossy recruitment ads. If you're a teacher, you'll find solidarity here in knowing you're not alone. If you're not, you'll gain a glimpse into the absurd, relentless grind that defines this profession.

PART

1

THE TEACHING JOURNEY – EXPECTATION VS REALITY

CHAPTER 1

THE ULTIMATE SURVIVAL TEST

Alright, buckle up. Imagine my life as a teacher, but instead of warm-hearted *Dead Poets Society* vibes, think *Black Mirror* meets *The Hunger Games,* with a sprinkle of dystopian comedy.

Picture this: I'm sprawled on my sofa, recovering from the trauma of another day, when an advert comes on the TV. It's got cheery music, stock photos of laughing students and an earnest voiceover about "inspiring the next generation". I quash the urge to hurl the remote control at the TV and yell, "Inspire? You mean endure, don't you?!" They paint teaching like it's *The Great British Bake Off,* but it's really more like the soggy cake left out in the rain.

Let's strip away the sugar-coating and get to the truth about teaching. The reality is not the smiling kids and noble speeches you see in adverts; it is a relentless grind where survival instincts matter more than your qualifications. Every day feels like a battle: managing overcrowded classrooms, enduring verbal abuse from students and parents, and navigating a system that seems to be designed to test your patience rather than your skills. "Inspire the next generation," they say. But nobody tells you that inspiration comes second to crowd control, or that half your day will be used up documenting every tiny incident to cover your back if complaints roll in.

Take a typical day in the classroom. Imagine 35 students squeezed into a room designed for 25, desks shoved against the walls, and the air heavy with simmering disruption. Two students have already been sent to the "reflection room" for using language that would make a football terrace blush, one is sulking at the back because their phone was confiscated, and following a break-time playground bust-up, another is halfway to a dramatic meltdown worthy of a soap opera. Forget pedagogy – you're playing behaviour manager, crisis negotiator and ringmaster all at once, in an environment where the rules seem to change every five minutes, and the inspection team might walk in just as someone launches a chair across the room.

No one prepares you for the emotional toll of the job. You're expected to maintain control, manage behavioural issues and keep up with constant administrative demands, all while trying to manage your own mental health. Add in the endless hours of marking, the pressure of maintaining discipline and the weight of ever-increasing expectations, it quickly becomes clear that teaching is not just about the knowledge that you're expected to impart to your students, but what you're required to endure yourself.

The advertisements promise you'll "make a difference". What they don't mention is that the difference you're likely to feel is in your stress levels and blood pressure. Teaching is akin to having a never-ending performance review where every mistake is magnified, every success overlooked, and every new initiative just adds to an already overwhelming workload.

TEACH, SURVIVE, REPEAT

This isn't the dream job they sell you. It's a system that strips away your passion and chips away at your mental health. And when you finally make it to the weekend, instead of rest, you're haunted by thoughts of Monday because, in teaching, the work never stops.

When I started teaching, I was full of the optimism that comes with a new career. I thought I'd walk into the classroom and change the world. I was fresh-faced, armed with innovative lesson ideas and eager to "make a difference". Fast forward 18 years and I've realised that teaching doesn't change the world — it just teaches you how to endure it.

But don't just take my word for it. Visit *Life After Teaching – Exit the Classroom and Thrive*, a Facebook group where the façade of teaching is stripped away and the truth revealed in raw, unfiltered posts. It's not just a support group — it's a lifeline. A place for educators to share their survival strategies, vent their frustrations and help each other cling to their sanity. If you think you're struggling, spend a few minutes scrolling through the posts and you'll see that teaching is less of a job and more of an endurance test. The stories shared here are not minor complaints; they're real, gut-wrenching accounts of burnout, stress and resilience, often mixed with dark humour and the occasional glimmer of hope.

The group offers teachers a space to come together to share their battle stories. These aren't casual gripes about heavy workloads or difficult students. They are gritty accounts from educators who've been pushed to their limits. False accusations, systemic issues and the overwhelming stress of the profession are common topics. Any teachers who even slightly slow down become the objects of scrutiny, with the system seemingly sensing exhaustion from a mile away. Before long, they're in "capability meetings", hearing phrases like "performance concerns", all while the system slowly erodes their careers.

Then come the accusations from parents – every teacher's worst nightmare. If Student X is told "no" in a classroom, suddenly you're responsible for his emotional trauma. Parents may accuse you of everything, from destroying their child's future to crushing their dreams.

Just when you think you've survived the onslaught, the realisation hits: if the parents and students don't target you, your colleagues might. Yes, there are teachers who would throw you under the bus in a heartbeat, driven by departmental politics. Backstabbing, sabotage and passive-aggressive emails turn the staffroom into a low-budget episode of *Succession*, but with fewer perks and more politics.

Then there's the administration. They'll leave you hanging, discredited and humiliated, all while feeding you lines like, "We're just doing what's best for the children". It's *Game of Thrones* with interactive whiteboards and Ofsted inspections – except the dragons are the SLT, whose decisions can burn your career to ashes with every accusation.

However, this group isn't just a place to vent; it's also a source of strength. Every post, every comment, every shared experience offers a lifeline to someone wondering if they're alone. It's proof that yes, this job can take a toll, but it also offers a reminder that there's life beyond the chaos. Sometimes that life is better, sometimes it's not – but knowing you're not alone in your struggles is powerful. If you're a teacher on the edge, questioning your choices and feeling like you're barely holding on, groups like this offer a chance to connect, share and understand that you're not just surviving – you're part of a community fighting to thrive.

When I started teaching in the early 2000s, I had a clear vision. I believed I would inspire young minds, broaden their horizons and open their eyes to the world. As a teaching assistant, I even had the opportunity to take a group of Black students from Tower Hamlets in East London to Ghana, documenting every step of the journey. That experience was transformative; the students returned with new outlooks on life. I also attended a retreat aimed at empowering Black and Asian middle leaders to break barriers and advance into senior roles. It was an inspiring initiative that gave me hope for real change in a system that desperately needed it. Standing there, listening to their ideas and vision, I thought – *This is it. This is the future of education. I want to be a part of this movement.*

So, I signed up for a PGCE course in Carlisle, convinced I was destined to teach ICT to the next generation. What I didn't know was that Carlisle would soon reveal the complex politics of the education system, all neatly packaged under the guise of "professional development".

On my first day, I walked into what I expected to be a typical school environment. But I quickly realised how mistaken I was. I found myself among 69 other trainees (yes, 70 of us) huddled together with bright eyes, notepads, and the naïve belief that we were about to make a difference. Why 70, you ask? Well, because the outgoing headteacher had hired us all in what could only be described as an ill-conceived parting "gift" for the incoming management. It was the educational equivalent of leaving a flaming bag of dog poo on someone's doorstep.

TEACH, SURVIVE, REPEAT

For context, most secondary schools typically take on 10–12 trainee teachers at a time. But 70? Seventy trainees was both laughable and tragic. We were everywhere – spilling out of staff rooms, perched on window ledges and queuing for the printer like it was the last working portaloo at a music festival. What was supposed to be "teacher training" quickly turned into a survival exercise.

Two months into my teaching career, I had a stark realisation: I didn't belong. The environment wasn't overtly hostile, but it was isolating in ways that words can't fully convey. As a Black man in an area where the only other Black face I saw was my own reflection in the school windows, I began to suspect that I wasn't thriving. It felt like attending a concert where none of the songs were familiar. That was my daily experience. The locals, lovely as they were, seemed perplexed by my presence – like I had turned up to a cricket match dressed for the Notting Hill Carnival.

So, I made the only logical decision: I packed my bags and returned to London, the city of crowded Tube carriages and overpriced coffee, where I could at least blend into the chaos. I decided to give teaching another try, this time enrolling in a PGCE course for Media and English. *How bad could it be?* I thought. Spoiler alert: it was considerably worse. But we'll get to that in due course.

Some teachers may turn these pages and think, "This doesn't reflect my experience at all." To those fortunate enough to feel that way, I offer my congratulations. You are among the rare few who have managed to steer clear of the harsher realities of the profession. For most of us, however, the experience is starkly different.

Should you ever find yourself deemed surplus to requirements by senior leadership, the hidden machinery begins to grind. Beneath the surface lies a complex web of disciplinary hearings, settlement agreements and eye-watering payouts, quietly diverting millions from already stretched education budgets.

According to the charity Education Support, bullying and harassment are all too prevalent in schools, yet such issues are often swept under the carpet. Teaching is far more than a profession; it's a daily battle – one filled with challenges that were conspicuously absent from those idealistic teacher recruitment campaigns.

CHAPTER 2

TEACHING IN HELL'S POSTCODE

Over my career I've been in various battlefields masquerading as classrooms; faith schools clinging to their last shred of piety, academies with glossy brochures masking chaos, and pupil referral units that felt one fire alarm away from a riot. But nothing prepared me for *this* school. If you want to know what teaching in purgatory feels like, I can give you the postcode. This wasn't just my worst teaching job – it was full-scale pandemonium. The kind of place that makes you question if anyone in charge actually knew what they were doing. Because here's the truth: the Senior Leadership Team had no control over the students. None. And it showed.

Every morning, I'd pull into the car park, my knuckles white on the steering wheel, staring into the abyss. I'd sit there, engine running, debating the logistics of a self-inflicted fender-bender. Not for drama, mind you – just enough to buy myself a trip to A&E and maybe, if I was lucky, a week off. Anything to delay walking into a building where the kids ruled the roost and the adults had long since surrendered power.

This wasn't a school; it was an unregulated circus. Forget behaviour policies; they were just words on paper, ignored as easily as a supply teacher. The students knew they were untouchable, and the SLT either didn't dare challenge them or simply didn't care. If Dante had been a teacher, this school would have inspired one of his circles of hell. It didn't need inspections or improvement plans; it needed divine intervention. Holy water? Bring a hosepipe. Exorcists? Assemble an army. Whatever it would take to cleanse a school where leadership had abandoned their post, leaving disorder to thrive unchecked.

The Students

The students were a force of nature: cursing, throwing things and starting fights as if it were a national sport. Whenever I tried to address their behaviour with management, I was met with a shrug and a cheery, "Well, it could be worse!". Worse? That would involve setting fire to the science labs as a prank or putting laxatives in the canteen food – and, come to think of it, they did both of those things.

I'm not new to teaching; I've handled tough crowds. But this group made me feel like a supply teacher on day one of my career. They could smell fear, and I was marinating in it. Let me take you through the highlights:

Class 1: The "Special" Year 10 Group

Class 1 consisted of nine Year 10 students, each with a list of challenges: ADHD, oppositional defiant disorder, emotional behaviour disorder – you name it. If Dante had encountered this group, he might have added a tenth circle of hell to his list.

The classroom was an art room, complete with paint, sharp tools and water; a veritable prop box for chaos. Within minutes of the lesson starting, one student would be standing on a table, another under my desk, and a third testing whether acrylic paint was flammable. Attempts to engage them with a book would invariably lead to them turning off the lights and chanting.

Support was non-existent. Despite countless calls for assistance, the SLT steered clear. At the end of each session, the students would grin as if they'd mastered the art of rebellion, and demand commendations. "You should thank us, sir; we didn't set the room on fire." In this school, that almost counted as good behaviour.

Class 2: The Year 8 House of Horrors

Then there was Class 2 – a group of Year 8s whose collective attitude could rival a rowdy mob of football hooligans. These weren't your run-of-the-mill teenagers; they treated school rules like suggestions, to be followed only if the mood struck them.

Lesson number one: never, under any circumstances, turn your back. One slip-up and you'd find mysterious fluids on the back of your shirt. Or worse. I quickly learned to check every seat before sitting down and wipe every door handle before touching it. This group didn't just argue; they would drag you into full-blown courtroom debates. The girls would disagree for sport, while the boys plotted ways to test my patience – and my survival instincts. Raising your voice was like lighting a fuse.

If a fight broke out, I had two choices: restrain someone, which could land me in hot water with safeguarding (these kids were actively looking for opportunities to make allegations about staff and get them fired), or leave the room, which would make it look like I was abandoning my duty. It was like keeping order in a zoo, but the animals weren't in cages and knew they had legal rights. The boys would climb out of windows, tear up textbooks and once, one of them even tried climbing into the ceiling tiles to avoid doing a detention. Meanwhile, the girls would encourage them, then feign innocence when it all went wrong.

Class 3: The Evil Year 10s

Finally, Class 3 – a full Year 10 class of 25 students. If my previous classes were challenging, this one pushed me to my limits. These students weren't just unruly; they were strategic. Every ounce of their energy and intelligence was weaponised against any semblance of order. Teaching here felt less like education and more like trench warfare.

Imagine standing at the front of the room, trying to deliver a lesson while the atmosphere simmers with hostility and malice. Turning to write on the board was a gamble – every time my back was turned, I invited a new act of defiance. Phones materialised, crisps crunched and students openly mocked the lesson. One day, someone brought in a full McDonald's meal and ate it like it was the most normal thing in the world.

The noise was relentless. Shouting, jeering, chairs being tipped back; I was in a pressure cooker with no release valve. The behaviour wasn't just disruptive, it was outright dangerous. Bullying was rampant and happening right under my nose while I desperately tried to keep control, but the perpetrators couldn't care less that I could see them. They knew there would be no repercussions. On one occasion, a fight broke out and I had to shout myself hoarse just to stop it. When I reported it to the SLT, the response was a shrug and a trite remark about "challenging environments". It was an unabashed abdication of responsibility.

Then came the humiliation. If I asked a student to sit down or issued some other innocuous instruction, the entire class would regularly burst into boos, as if I was a pantomime villain. Once, a student answered a phone call mid-lesson, chatting away while I stood there dumbfounded. Another time, a parent called their child during class and when I instructed the student to put their phone away, the parent began shouting at me (on speakerphone) using a range of expletives to inform me that I had no right to stop them from speaking to their child. It was anarchy.

Breaking Point

Every morning, I sat in my car psyching myself up, asking, "Is the pay really worth this?" Most days, the answer was no.

I didn't last long there. I couldn't. The place started invading my dreams – nightmares about being locked in the classroom by Class 3 while alarms blared, and chaos reigned. Leaving wasn't a decision – it was an act of self-preservation. By the time I handed in my resignation, I wasn't thinking about what came next. I was simply trying to escape.

A System Built on Exploitation

Here's the truly harrowing part: I wasn't the exception. The staff turnover at that school was astronomical. It wasn't just a revolving door; it was a vortex. Many teachers weren't even British. They'd been recruited from countries like Jamaica, South Africa and Australia, on temporary visas. Trapped by the terms of their employment, they had no choice but to endure, knowing that leaving meant risking their immigration status. It was exploitation, pure and simple, and management relied on it to keep the school running.

One Jamaican teacher who I still keep in touch with is stuck there, waiting for his visa to expire. Every conversation with him feels like a plea for help. He talks about the emotional toll of being worn down by the daily verbal and physical abuse he faces. At one point he was the focus of a targeted campaign of racial abuse by three Year 11s whose behaviour was repeatedly excused because "their exams are in a few months, so they'll be leaving soon". He's appalled by the way that behaviour which would be deemed to be criminal in the public domain, is tolerated and goes unpunished within school walls.

The Bigger Picture

This isn't an isolated story. There are schools like this across the UK, where the system is so broken that the idea of "education" is almost laughable. It's not about learning; it's about endurance. For many, there's no way out. Schools like these are often located in areas of high deprivation and attract teachers who are either desperate for a job or naive enough to think they can make a difference. By the time they comprehend the reality, they're already trapped – financially, emotionally or even legally, as with the foreign teachers on employment visas.

But the real victims are the students. These chaotic environments don't just harm teachers, they fail the children. The students who truly want to learn, who crave structure and stability, are left to fend for themselves in institutions that prioritise containment over education.

And when Ofsted arrives, the illusion takes over. The chaos is hidden, problem students are given "study days" or taken on strategic school trips and teachers are reminded to "focus on the positives". It's a farce.

The Trauma of Leaving

By the time I left, I wasn't angry, I was numb. Numb to the excuses, the deflections and the endless cycle of disorder and damage that management not only allowed but perpetuated. Leaving felt like waking up from a bad dream. But even now, the memories linger. Sometimes I'll drive past that school and feel a wave of dread, as if I'm about to step back into that car park for another day in hell. It's a trauma that stays with you, a reminder of just how broken the system can be.

CHAPTER

3

THE COST OF CARING

Teaching is a profession with a complex and often hidden reality. It's not uncommon for teachers to become the subject of conversations at social gatherings, with people leaning in as if they're hearing the latest episode of a true-crime podcast. "Wow, that's brave of you," they say, as if describing time spent in a war zone. Or "I couldn't do what you do", which often comes across as a polite way of saying, "I'd rather not". Then, there are those who couldn't continue – teachers who left the profession after a few years, or sometimes just long enough to realise the "calling" was more of a voicemail they should have ignored. These aren't stories of mild dissatisfaction – they're accounts of people who felt their spirits gradually eroded by relentless bureaucracy, toxic politics and the emotional demands of a profession that takes everything, then asks for more.

When someone asks, "Why don't you just leave?" the answer is rarely simple. Initially, idealism keeps teachers in the classroom. They believe they are making a difference, that the system is salvageable, and that things will improve if they just hold on a little longer. But as time passes, the reality sets in. Teachers progress through the pay scale, but the incremental raises are often outpaced by inflation, leaving many facing real-term pay cuts and struggling financially. Nevertheless, it's a stable income, so they persevere and by the time they hit their forties, many realise that teaching has become more than just a job; it has become their identity, influencing how they think, interact with others and process stress. Leaving the profession would mean starting over, often in a role that doesn't come close to matching their experience or income. For many, the fear of losing that financial stability and the daunting prospect of reinventing themselves keeps them locked in a system that extracts and drains, while offering just enough to make them stay.

Here's what that reality looks like – heartbreaking stories from teachers who have lived it:

One teacher, an experienced professional with decades of service, was suddenly called into a meeting with no warning and no representation. They were handed a "support plan" with unrealistic targets and an impossible timeline – just four teaching days to comply, due to part-time hours. In spite of the name, there was no support offered. This wasn't about improvement and the message was clear: leave or be forced out. As the sole earner in their household, the teacher was crushed, caught between the pressure of a toxic workplace and the fear of losing everything. The emotional toll was devastating, and the irony was even more galling. If this teacher had treated any of their students in this way, they would have been accused of bullying and undoubtedly been subjected to disciplinary procedures.

Then there's the story of one senior leader who joined the profession full of optimism, eager to make a difference. But as complaints mounted and the stress took its toll, her personal life began to unravel. Her partner, frustrated by her unreasonable working hours, told her that they would need to put plans for expanding their family on hold. Now the union is involved, but all she can do is wait in uncertainty, fearing that every decision could be the wrong one. "I'm broken," she confides. From her demeanour it's clear that the system has drained her, leaving her with little hope for a better future.

Another teacher, a young mother, returned to work after maternity leave, trying to balance the needs of her newborn with a demanding teaching schedule. But the passion she once had was gone, buried beneath piles of ungraded work and sleepless nights. Her exam groups were reassigned "for the good of the students," she was told. But what about her? She's exhausted, teetering on the edge of burnout, and now her counsellor warns her that she is at risk of collapse. She dreams of leaving, of finding a job that doesn't feel like a daily marathon, but the financial reality keeps her trapped in a profession she once loved. She isn't alone – recent data from *The Guardian* reveals that women aged 30 to 39, many of whom are mothers with young children, represent the largest demographic leaving teaching annually, with over 9,000 exiting the profession in 2022–3 due to many factors including inflexible working conditions.[i] While some are unable to leave their jobs for financial reasons, with the rising cost of childcare and comparatively stagnant teacher salaries, this may no longer be the case moving forward, suggesting even more losses from a profession once prized as a good option for those with young families.

Another teacher, nearing retirement, was accused of gross misconduct based on a fabricated story from a student. He spent four agonising months wondering if his 29-year career was about to end over an unfounded accusation. Despite union support, the hearing was a formality, and his side was barely considered. In the end, he received a warning, but the emotional damage was done. The experience left him with a constant sense of vulnerability, always fearing the next accusation.

These stories are all too common. Teachers are left to navigate a system that seems designed to punish rather than support. Many joined unions hoping for advocacy, only to find that school policies are cleverly used against them. Union representatives, overwhelmed and under-resourced, are often unable to provide meaningful support. Instead, teachers are left alone, facing a labyrinth of bureaucracy, with accusations and hearings that make them feel as though they are always on the verge of dismissal.

False accusations from students have become increasingly common, with teachers finding themselves facing investigations over misunderstandings so trivial they border on absurdity. Meanwhile, the union files grow thicker, and the letters from school leadership become more ominous. Teachers begin to feel as though they are being targeted, their careers hanging by a thread.

Teachers have spoken openly in staffrooms about feeling isolated and trapped, their mental health unravelling due to the weight of the workload and other pressures of the profession. Some have even reached the point of considering suicide. One teacher shared a post online after a disciplinary hearing, revealing that they had considered ending their life. The outcome of the hearing was that they were deemed to require a minor "training need", but the experience left them emotionally scarred, their dignity stripped away, and their sense of self shattered.

TEACH, SURVIVE, REPEAT

Every day, more stories emerge of teachers grappling with stress, sleeplessness and panic attacks. They face systemic bullying from senior leadership teams, the weaponisation of policies and constant scrutiny. Bit by bit, they are worn down until there is nothing left to give. Many are signed off sick, investigated, and – if they're 'lucky' – quietly dismissed with a settlement that barely covers the cost of therapy. Those who leave teaching often carry emotional scars that make it impossible to trust another workplace again.

So, when people ask us at gatherings, "How do you manage?", the truth, sadly, is that many of us don't. For every teacher still holding on, countless others have been broken by the relentless pressure and the emotional toll of trying to survive in a system that feels designed to wear you down. We begin with hope, with passion, with the belief that we can make a difference. But too often, we are chewed up and spat out, left to pick up the pieces of ourselves in a world that doesn't acknowledge the cost.

Teaching isn't just a job; it's a gauntlet. And for those of us who make it out, we carry the scars. But even though we are haunted by what we've been through and may wish to forget, we have a responsibility to speak out, to share our stories and to reveal the truth about what it's really like. Because perhaps, just maybe, if enough people hear these stories, things will finally change.

PART 2
SYSTEMIC FAILURES – A BROKEN SYSTEM

CHAPTER 4

EDUCATION INC.: THE CORPORATE TAKEOVER

When I started teaching nearly 20 years ago, education was about the children. It was about curiosity, exploration and preparing them to enter the adult world with confidence and critical thinking skills. Today, in many schools, teaching feels more like working on the production line of an exam factory. The joy of learning has been replaced by the grind of meeting performance metrics, and the ethos of education for its own sake has been sacrificed to the cold, hard drive for efficiency.

Many schools no longer function as institutions of learning but as businesses, with academies leading this transformation. Multi-academy trusts (MATs), which oversee multiple schools, operate like corporate franchises. Their focus on expansion, branding and cost-cutting often neglects the needs of students and teachers.

In many academy trusts, the management structure resembles that of a business. CEOs lead MATs, earning eye-watering six-figure salaries to oversee schools from afar. For example, in 2023, the CEO of one of the largest academy chains in the UK earned over £250,000 per year. Meanwhile, classroom teachers, who work directly with students, face pay freezes and resource shortages.

One science teacher remarked, "Our CEO earns more in a month than our entire department's annual budget. Meanwhile, I'm rationing photocopying paper and buying pens out of my own pocket."

These CEOs are often far removed from the realities of teaching. Decisions are centralised, with policies handed down to individual schools that must comply regardless of their unique challenges. A headteacher, once the cornerstone of a school community, now functions more like a middle manager, implementing and enforcing directives from above.

Another teacher noted, "Our head used to know every student's name. Now, they spend more time in meetings about data than walking through the corridors, so some of the newer children don't even know what they look like."

Disposable Teachers in the Academy Era

In many schools, short-term contracts have become the norm, particularly for new teachers. These six-month probationary contracts are framed as an opportunity to "test the fit", but they often exploit staff. Teachers are given little support and feel under constant scrutiny, with the threat of non-renewal hanging over them.

One teacher shared their frustration: "I spent my first term terrified of being let go. I focused so much on meeting management's expectations that I barely had time to build relationships with my students."

Temporary leadership roles, such as some TLRs (Teaching and Learning Responsibilities), are another source of frustration for many staff. These roles are handed out with the expectation of delivering rapid results, only to be unceremoniously withdrawn if unrealistic targets aren't met. "It feels like we're being used," said one teacher. "You take on extra work and stress for a year, and then they pull it all away because your results didn't jump high enough, even if progress was made."

Overcrowded Classrooms, Underfunded Schools

In many schools, efficiency has become the overriding priority. This focus on cost-cutting has led to overcrowded classrooms, with some teachers managing more than 35 students in a single room. Basic resources, such as textbooks and stationery, are in short supply, forcing teachers to dip into their own pockets or turn to crowdfunding.

One teacher recounted: "I've taught lessons where students had to sit on the floor because there weren't enough chairs. How can anyone expect quality teaching and learning in those conditions?"

Even essential infrastructure is neglected in some schools. Another teacher shared: "Our heating broke down last winter, and we taught in coats for weeks. But the academy still found money for a new promotional video for the trust's website".

Support staff cuts have compounded the problem, leaving teachers to manage SEND students and behavioural issues with little to no help. A secondary school teacher explained, "I'm expected to plan, differentiate and manage behaviour for 35 students, all while logging data and responding to emails. It's impossible".

The Disappearance of Subjects

Many schools have adopted the business model of cutting "unprofitable" subjects. A-level and post-16 courses with low enrolment figures are frequently axed, even if they are vital for a well-rounded education. Creative subjects such as music, drama and media studies are often the first to go.

One teacher expressed their dismay: "Our school dropped media A-level because only seven students signed up. It didn't matter that those seven students were talented and passionate – the numbers just weren't high enough."

Students are being pushed into studying subjects that boost league table scores rather than align with their interests or talents. Another teacher noted: "We're funnelling kids into courses they hate, just to make the data look better. Their interests or aspirations don't factor into it."

The Tyranny of Data

In most schools, data now dictates every aspect of teaching. Teachers are expected to spend hours inputting grades, analysing trends and creating action plans to "close gaps" in performance. This relentless focus on numbers leaves little room for creativity or adapting lessons to individual student needs. One teacher shared: "I spend more time filling out spreadsheets than actually teaching. It's like the kids have become secondary to the data."

The pressure to meet targets also leads to questionable practices. Another teacher explained, "We're told to focus on students who are just below the grade boundary because they'll have the biggest impact on our statistics. Everyone else gets sidelined." Similarly, in another school which had recently become part of a MAT, teachers were told not to focus their energy on or offer interventions to recent additions to the cohort, such as students who joined mid-year due to being refugees or asylum seekers. This was because their results wouldn't count towards the progess data, so there was no point offering them the support they needed to develop and thrive. Nevermind that some of these students were desperate to learn and assimilate into a new community that they had been thrust into due to often quite harrowing circumstances. But empathy or compassion has no place in these exam factories, where children are not viewed as people, but only valued according to the data they represent at the end of a key stage.

The Marketing Machine

Many academies are skilled at marketing. Open days are polished productions, complete with glossy brochures, staged displays and professional videos. Social media accounts are filled with curated posts showing smiling students and sparkling facilities, masking the struggles behind the scenes.

A teacher observed: "Our academy spends thousands on marketing materials, but we can't afford new textbooks for our GCSE students. It's all about looking good, not being good."

This obsession with optics diverts resources from where they're needed most. Another teacher noted: "Our trust spent a fortune rebranding every school, but we still don't have enough laptops for students who need them. They've also let go half the support staff in our school, so students with additional learning needs no longer have the access to classroom support that they require in order to engage effectively in lessons."

Silencing Passionate Teachers

The truth is, the system doesn't want passionate, dedicated teachers. It doesn't want people who care too much or think too deeply about the impact they could have. What it wants is compliance. It wants teachers who will stay in their lane, follow the rules, meet the targets, and not ask too many questions. It wants us exhausted, ground down and too worn out to push back. It wants to mute our objections, despite their validity.

So, we do as we're told. We smile, nod and drag ourselves back to work each day, knowing full well the toll it takes on our health, our happiness and our lives.

Tomorrow, thousands of us will wake up, brace ourselves, and resume the daily grind. We'll pour our hearts into our work, hoping for those rare moments of connection with students that remind us why we started. Hoping to make a difference and improve a child's life chances. And we do all this *in spite of*, not with the support of, a system that cares more about data and the illusion of perfection than it does about individual students or staff. It's a business, a corporate machine with no empathy or soul, just the constant demand for more. Always more.

CHAPTER

5

PASS AT ANY COST

Cheating – it's the word no one wants to say out loud, yet every teacher, headteacher and caretaker in the school system knows it happens. It may not occur everywhere, but it's more prevalent than many would like to admit. It's the Voldemort of education: feared, never discussed and casting a shadow over every exam room. And as for grade inflation? That's as common as cold tea in the staffroom.

So, here's the uncomfortable truth: those certificates that some students walk away with are not always as deserved as they appear. If you've ever met a teenager who holds a clutch of GCSEs but thinks Shakespeare is a footballer, you've probably encountered the reality of grade inflation. You might find yourself asking, "If he has a grade 7 in English Language, why does he think 'there', 'their' and 'they're' are interchangeable?"

The Pressure Cooker of Targets

It all starts with targets. Departments, schools and entire academies are judged on how many students obtain certain grades, with the SLT treating target grades like a sacred goal. And if a student's English target is a grade 7, but their greatest literary achievement is finishing *The Gruffalo*, what's a teacher to do? Tell the truth and risk failing their own performance review? Or turn a blind eye to a few…creative methods?

Teachers don't want to be part of a grade-inflating system, but the reality is that no one wants their performance evaluations to resemble a crime report. According to *The Times*, over 80% of teachers feel pressured to meet inflated targets, even when faced with students who think *Hamlet* is about a talking piglet. So, do you give them the grade and move on? Or risk a performance improvement plan for suggesting that maybe *Great Expectations* isn't "boring" and they should at least give it a try?

When Teachers Look the Other Way

Let's talk about reality. After the pandemic, I witnessed cheating like never before. 2021 became the year of "open-book exams" … with Google, Bing and occasionally Siri acting as the real examination companions. It was as if exams had turned into a game show, with students phoning friends and consulting every lifeline possible. Teachers became aware of students openly Googling answers, others with slips of paper hidden in their pencil cases, and even one who claimed his Apple Watch was just for "checking the time".

The most outrageous example of cheating has to be the student who managed to slip his actual exam paper into the wrong pile, take it home for a late-night review and then return it with revised answers, leading to a grade 6 in English.

And then there were the "home exams" during the pandemic. In one school, students known for refusing to attend classes were handed entire GCSE papers to complete at their convenience. These were students who hadn't set foot in a classroom in months yet somehow returned nearly perfect responses. When a few of us raised concerns, we were met with a shrug and a nod, as if to say, "We're all in this together… to make the numbers look good."

Plagiarism, Copy-Pasting and the Vocational Circus

The growth of digital education means that plagiarism has never been easier. I once had a vocational student who submitted coursework that looked suspiciously well-written and after some investigation I discovered that it was her older sister's work from the previous year. I reported it, expecting a serious discussion about academic integrity, but the response was a shrug and a "let's give her another chance". By the end of the term, the student had her grade, her sister had a laugh and I had a few more grey hairs.

It's not just vocational students either. GCSE students are also taking shortcuts. With the internet at their fingertips, they've become copy-pasting experts. *Pride and Prejudice* essays magically appear overnight, identical to the ones found on SparkNotes, and yet some parents still claim their child did the research themselves. Really? Little Alfie, who thinks a thesaurus is a dinosaur, suddenly starts writing about "epistolary techniques" like an Oxford graduate?

The Maths Just Doesn't Add Up

Ever notice how, every year, more students seem to be achieving grade 7-9, yet literacy rates in the real world remain embarrassingly low? According to Ofqual, GCSE pass rates have steadily climbed[ii], but basic literacy levels haven't budged. So, where are all these high grades coming from? Either Charles

Dickens has risen from his grave to tutor the next generation or something is seriously wrong.

Employers have noticed this too. Over 40% of employers report that school leavers lack the basic skills needed for work.

When Teachers Pay the Price

It's not just the students who suffer in this farce. Teachers who dare to call out cheating or grade inflation are often met with a backlash. Ever had a meeting with an angry parent who insists their child's "totally unique" essay wasn't copied from Wikipedia? Or tried explaining to a line manager why you can't, in good conscience, give a student a grade 7 in English when they've spent most of the year thinking a simile is a smiling yellow emoji?

Standing up to this corruption can feel like career suicide. Management will tell you that, "it's your responsibility to handle it quietly" – meaning, don't rock the boat, just pass them. And when you try to uphold academic integrity, you're often treated like you're ruining the student's future, rather than helping them avoid embarrassment further down the road.

The Fallout – When Inflated Grades Meet Reality

The harsh reality is that this grade inflation sets students up for a rude awakening once they leave school. Many sail through their GCSEs, believing they've mastered key subjects, only to find themselves woefully unprepared for the demands of further education, apprenticeships, or the workplace. Employers frequently raise concerns about the so-called "skills gap," as though it's an enigma, when in truth, it's the predictable outcome of a system more focused on performance data than genuine learning.

The Confederation of British Industry (CBI) has repeatedly reported that school leavers lack essential skills, particularly in literacy, and it's easy to see why. When a student can achieve a grade 6 in English without understanding what a metaphor is, we're all in trouble.[iii]

So, What's the Solution?

If we're going to fix this mess, it's going to take more than just putting up a "No Cheating" sign in the exam hall. We need a system where teachers aren't forced to choose between their integrity and their job, where academic honesty is valued over polished performance reports. We need to ensure that students graduate with skills they can actually apply, rather than a string of inflated grades that hold no real value for employers.

Until then, the cycle of inflated grades, stressed teachers and confused employers will only continue. And if you're ever surprised by a CV with an impressive spread of GCSEs, only to find an email riddled with grammatical errors, just remember: those grades were probably more of a "team effort" than an individual achievement.

CHAPTER 6

THE DESTRUCTIVE OFSTED MACHINE

In March 2023, the teaching community was shaken by the tragic death of Ruth Perry, a headteacher who took her own life after her school was downgraded from "Outstanding" to "Inadequate" by Ofsted. Her death was a brutal reminder of the crushing weight of inspections – how schools, leaders and teachers are not judged on their actual value to the communities they serve, but on cold, clinical metrics. Ruth Perry's death wasn't an isolated tragedy; it was a stark warning of what happens when accountability becomes a weapon wielded without care.

The Call That Changes Everything

For schools, the Ofsted call is the moment everything stops. With barely a day's notice – sometimes just a few hours – the machinery of education grinds to a halt, replaced by an all-consuming scramble to prepare. Plans are abandoned, evenings are sacrificed, and lessons, once deemed sufficient, are rewritten in a frantic attempt to meet an ever-shifting standard. Leadership teams huddle in urgent meetings, scripting their "narrative", while teachers rehearse their roles, transforming their classrooms into theatres of compliance. The focus shifts, abruptly and unequivocally, from nurturing young minds to orchestrating a façade.

This transformation often borders on the absurd. Problematic students vanish, sent to alternative provisions or taken on impromptu "educational visits", conveniently off-site during the inspection window. Some are even "encouraged" to stay at home on sanctioned days off to keep them out of sight. Behaviour policies that are inconsistently applied on regular days are suddenly enforced with military precision, creating a version of school life that inspectors are meant to see – not the reality experienced by staff and students.

Teachers are handed scripts, painstakingly rehearsing answers to anticipated questions. They are sternly reminded not to mention workload, ongoing struggles, or anything that might tarnish the carefully curated image. One teacher described the chaos: "I was told to completely rewrite my lesson plan at 6 p.m. because it wasn't 'Ofsted-ready.' It had worked perfectly for months, but that didn't matter. It wasn't good enough for the show."

Even students are coached to play their part. A secondary teacher recounted: "We were instructed to 'remind' kids to be respectful, make eye contact and always say they're enjoying lessons. One kid laughed and asked if they were supposed to lie. We didn't have an answer."

The inspection becomes a performance, choreographed to impress. The inspectors seem oblivious to the chaos in the wings, the tears of exhaustion in the staffroom or the students hidden from view because they might tarnish the illusion.

For many, this process is more than disruptive; it's devastating. On an online teaching forum, a headteacher, worn down by years of relentless scrutiny, admitted through tears, "In the middle of Ofsted, I was broken – utterly broken by a system that's impossible to sustain. I knew I couldn't do this anymore."

This isn't an isolated sentiment. Across the profession, fear of failure looms large, casting a shadow over even the most resilient educators. Another teacher wrote on the same forum, recounting their school's catastrophic inspection: "We failed Ofsted spectacularly – leadership was fragmented, teaching inconsistent. They turned us into an academy. A week later, an advisor came for a walkaround and said, 'Yes, the report is fair.' I can't explain the shame. Some mornings, I cry on my way to work."

When teachers are weeping in their cars, when headteachers feel they have no choice but to leave the profession, when schools are reshaped or erased on the basis of a two-day judgment, it's impossible to deny the destructive impact of Ofsted. It has taken a profession built on hope and learning and turned it into one ruled by fear.

In the aftermath of Ruth Perry's death, media coverage cast a spotlight on the outrageous and inhumane methods used by Ofsted. Stories of schools paralysed by fear, leaders blindsided by downgrades and teachers crushed under impossible standards flooded the public discourse. The nation could no longer ignore the brutal toll these inspections took on educators.

In response, Ofsted made some changes, albeit under intense pressure rather than the organic desire for genuine reform. Amongst these was the frequently requested removal of single word judgements, a system that had reduced the complexities of a school's efforts into reductive labels like "Outstanding" or "Inadequate." The change aimed to offer a more comprehensive understanding of a school's strengths and areas for development, replacing damaging headlines with a fuller narrative.

Other adjustments followed, including promises to consider context more thoughtfully, such as schools with high proportions of SEND pupils or those facing socio-economic challenges. Safeguarding practices, often weaponised as deal-breakers during inspections, were to be assessed with greater care.

Yet, for many in education, these changes felt perfunctory – a bandage over a deep wound. The structural flaws in the inspection system, driven by compliance and data above all else, remain largely unaddressed. While the removal of single word judgements signalled progress, it did little to ease the pervasive anxiety or repair the fractured trust between Ofsted and schools.

Clueless Inspectors

One of the most galling aspects of Ofsted inspections is the lack of expertise demonstrated by some inspectors. Decisions that can dismantle schools and end careers are made by individuals who often lack a fundamental understanding of the areas they are inspecting.

One teacher shared a shocking experience: "I sat in a Shropshire pub having a meal. On a nearby table were two couples. One couple was an Ofsted inspector and his headteacher wife. The other couple were an Ofsted inspector and his non-teaching wife. They loudly discussed and laughed at how they made their decisions. One said, 'I got landed with inspecting Early Years, which I know nothing about! I had to chat to my niece, who is an EYFS teacher, to find out about it.'"

The idea that an inspector with no knowledge of Early Years education could hold a school's fate in their hands is infuriating. It exemplifies the system's disregard for expertise, replacing it with a box-ticking exercise that prioritises inspection targets over understanding. Another teacher remarked, "It beggars belief that this is an example of an Ofsted inspector's lack of knowledge. I hope to goodness he didn't inspect your school's EYFS!"

For schools, this lack of knowledge is more than a source of frustration – it's a potential death sentence. Inspectors arrive with little understanding of the nuances of teaching or the challenges faced by specific departments and key stages. Their decisions often rely on surface impressions and assumptions rather than a developed, informed perspective.

The Fallout of Failure

For schools that receive a damning Ofsted report, the consequences are profound and far-reaching. A single inspection can trigger forced academisation, public humiliation, and a mass exodus of staff. Morale collapses almost overnight, and the shockwaves extend to every corner of the school community. In some cases, the financial stability of the school is jeopardised, further destabilising already precarious institutions. Years of hard-won progress can be wiped out in an instant, leaving educators and students to navigate the rubble of reputations and trust.

One teacher vividly described the aftermath: "Morale was already low, but after the report, it was like someone had died. Teachers were crying in the staffroom. Some handed in their notice the same week. It felt like the end." These aren't isolated accounts. They are the lived realities of a profession weighed down by a system that prioritises judgement over support and compliance over care.

This is not an exaggeration. It is a brutal truth. The Ofsted report card, supposedly designed to drive improvement, often functions as an instrument of dismantlement. Beyond damaging professional reputations, it erodes trust, shatters community confidence and leaves schools in chaos. Rather than fostering meaningful change, it creates a culture of fear where survival becomes the goal, not progress.

The veneer of rigorous auditing conceals deep flaws. Schools are judged on rigid, surface-level criteria that fail to account for the complexities of modern education – socio-economic challenges, the diverse needs of pupils and the critical pastoral work that forms the foundation of genuine progress. These omissions reduce schools to data points and labels, stripping away the humanity and nurturing qualities of teaching.

If this punitive approach continues unchecked, the cost will be devastating. Careers will be destroyed, mental health sacrificed and the futures of countless children jeopardised. The cracks in this system can no longer be ignored or papered over. A fundamental rethink of school accountability is urgently required – one that shifts the focus from punishment to partnership, from judgement to support, and from fear to growth.

Education should be a force for empowerment and transformation, not destruction. Inspections must evolve into tools for collaboration, driven by a shared goal of improvement. Anything less will continue to fail not just the schools, but the children and communities they serve.

CHAPTER 7
UNQUALIFIED TAKEOVER

I'm watching it happen. Right now. Right in front of me.

The profession I've spent my life building is being dismantled – brick by brick, role by role – until there's almost nothing left. It's not loud. It's not dramatic. It's slow. Silent. Insidious.

Teachers aren't being outright dismissed – that would draw too much attention. Instead, they're being quietly phased out, replaced by roles that cost less and require fewer qualifications. Jobs once held by fully trained teachers are being rebranded, downgraded, and handed to HLTAs (Higher Level Teaching Assistants) and staff with no formal teaching qualifications.

I'm not referring to the HLTAs who are former qualified teachers and have chosen to step back; it's about those without Qualified Teacher Status (QTS) being asked to deliver lessons, plan schemes of work and even assess pupils. While schools may claim these roles are 'supervised' by qualified teachers, the reality is far murkier. The distinction between support and teaching is being deliberately blurred. As one HLTA shared in a Facebook group, "I am an HLTA and I am timetabled to teach 5 50-minute lessons a week."iv

But we see it. We see it every single day. And it's breaking us.

It used to be straightforward. If you wanted to be a teacher, you trained. You earned your QTS through rigorous study and practice. You spent years learning about pedagogy, behaviour management, safeguarding, and how to strike the delicate balance between nurturing and challenging young minds. You completed your time as an NQT, steadily building your expertise with the hope of one day stepping into senior roles.

That's how it used to be. But now, the landscape is shifting rapidly.

I watch as positions like Head of Year and Curriculum Lead are quietly rebranded. "Learning Facilitator." "Pastoral Mentor." "HLTA Team Lead." On the surface, it seems harmless, just a new name or a reshuffle of responsibilities. But it's not harmless. It's a calculated move. These roles, once reserved for experienced teachers, are now filled by unqualified staff on significantly lower pro-rata salaries. No QTS required. No extensive training needed.

I've seen good teachers – brilliant teachers – pour their hearts into their roles, only to be passed over for promotion opportunities they were perfect for, due to financial reasons. Those jobs still exist, but they are given a different title in order to justify appointing non-teaching staff in those positions. For example, the pastoral role of 'Assistant Head of Year', which would typically have been offered to a member of teaching staff, is re-branded as 'Pastoral Support Officer' and offered to support staff instead, thereby removing a long-standing pathway of progression for teachers in order to reduce payroll costs.

Claire, an ex-colleague of mine, experienced a similar scenario. She'd been at her school for 10 years, working towards Head of

Year 11. She'd been leading interventions, mentoring students, and staying late to build her case. When the position finally became available following the departure of the previous Head of Year, it wasn't advertised under the same job title, but instead was listed as 'Pastoral Lead (Support Staff)'. Half the salary, no QTS required, no option for teaching staff to apply. The role was filled by an HLTA. I'll never forget the look on her face that day. That was the moment she checked out.

Let's be clear. HLTAs are not the problem and I am not attributing any blame to them in these circumstances. They've been put in an impossible position too. They were meant to be assistants; supporting teachers by helping small groups of students and running interventions etc. They were not meant to teach full classes. But when you can pay an HLTA £15,000 less than a teacher to deliver lessons on their own, suddenly "support" becomes "lead".

I've seen it happen. You walk past a classroom and see an HLTA teaching Year 9 Maths. Not covering – teaching. There is no qualified teacher in the room. No QTS. No formal training. Just a support worker doing their best to fill a role they were never supposed to have. The pressure on them is enormous. They're just trying to survive too. The school doesn't care though; they've done their own calculations. They can save £10,000, even £20,000, for every HLTA they put in front of a classroom instead of a qualified practitioner. It is not about education or providing students with a professional who has been trained to teach them the subject material. It's about the bottom line.

In secondary schools, the shortage of teachers in Mathematics, Science, and Computing has reached crisis point. Schools can't recruit qualified teachers, so they've stopped trying. Instead, they hire anyone with a vaguely relevant degree and call them

"Subject Specialists". Some of these "teachers" have as little as 6 weeks of training through schemes like Teach First or Subject Knowledge Enhancement (SKE).

You wouldn't know it. Parents don't know it. They hear "Your child's teacher is Mr Jones." They assume "teacher" means qualified, trained, experienced. It doesn't. Not anymore.

I'm watching good people walk away every term. People who should have been Lead Practitioners, Heads of Year, Curriculum Leaders. People who worked for years to climb a ladder that was quietly dismantled behind their backs.

I'm watching teachers being told to train the unqualified people who are replacing them. I'm watching HLTAs replace teachers and teachers become ghosts. I'm watching parents place their trust in schools that are quietly substituting experienced staff for unqualified strangers.

One day, parents will ask, "Where are all the teachers?" They'll look around and realise that the faces have changed. But by then, it'll be too late.

The teachers will be gone.

CHAPTER 8

THE PARENT TRAP

> "Teaching: a profession where you're tasked with shaping futures, fostering growth, and – let's be honest – navigating landmines disguised as parent-teacher interactions."
>
> "The Education of a Teacher: A Journey of Growth, Resilience, and Landmines" by Dr. Maria Thompson.

Every teacher undertakes their role with the hope of fostering a collaborative partnership with parents. But all too often, what should be a united front feels more like a battlefield. Expectations clash, frustrations escalate, and the shared goal of supporting the child gets lost amidst the tension. While there are moments of genuine cooperation, the reality for many educators is a series of interactions that feel more akin to a courtroom drama than constructive dialogue.

Take the example of a student in my Year 7 form group. At the beginning of the academic year, this pupil racked up twenty behavioural incidents in just four weeks. Naturally, I contacted his parent, anticipating concern and a willingness to work together to address the issues. What I encountered instead was a defensive rebuke. Rather than acknowledge that her son needed to do better, she responded with an instruction for me – "You need to build a rapport with him" – as though a casual chat or a bit of banter with me would magically transform this pupil into a model student. She also objected to my use of the term "behavioural issues", claiming it was inappropriate. Let's be clear: I wasn't opposed to talking to him and "building a rapport". In fact, we already had a fairly positive relationship. However, this clearly wasn't deterring him from misbehaving in a number of different classes. As a new student in his first year of secondary school, it was also important to establish clear behavioural expectations and ensure that this message was reinforced at home. But as this was clearly not happening, his poor behaviour continued, and when I contacted home again, as was my duty as his form tutor, his mother continued to deflect and attribute blame elsewhere rather than encourage him to take some accountability.

Sadly, this experience is not uncommon. A National Education Union (NEU) survey found that "57% of teachers have experienced verbal abuse from parents" – not just criticism or questioning, but outright hostility. Often, these confrontations arise from trivial matters that have been blown out of proportion, or school staff simply carrying out their duties, yet this does not deter some parents from attacking them.

A TES survey found that "20% of teachers actively avoid contacting parents due to fear of confrontation." These endless battles erode morale, contributing to the exodus of teachers from the profession.

The "Blamers" and "Justifiers"

The behaviour exhibited in the examples above leads some educators to categorise these 'problem' parents into two distinctive groups – the "blamers", who are quick to point fingers at anyone but their child, and the "justifiers", who specialise in reframing even the most egregious behaviour as a misunderstanding.

One particularly memorable case where both blame and justification was utilised by parents occurred when two Year 10 boys broke into a girls' bathroom and smeared faeces on the walls. It wasn't just an act of defiance; it was outright vandalism, leaving staff and pupils shocked by the extent of their actions. Naturally, the boys were suspended, and the school community expected their parents to treat the incident with the seriousness it deserved. Instead, the parents claimed the boys were being "unfairly targeted", dismissing the act as "just a prank" that had been blown out of proportion. In their view, the school's response was too harsh, and they argued that their children were victims of a system that didn't understand "boys being boys".

Against all logic and evidence, the school leaders faced mounting pressure to reintegrate the boys. Within weeks, they were back in class, strutting through the halls as if nothing had happened. The message to other pupils was clear: actions don't always have consequences, and with the right parental intervention, even the most serious offences could be brushed aside.

This isn't an isolated case. A 2021 TES survey revealed that "one in five teachers reported parents defending clear rule-breaking." These incidents undermine school policies and send conflicting messages to pupils about accountability and respect.

Helicopter and Snowplough Parenting

Hovering parents take on many forms. Helicopter parents micromanage every detail of their child's education, while snowplough parents bulldoze every challenge from their child's path. According to Dr. Wendy Mogel, clinical psychologist and author, these approaches undermine children's resilience. She writes, "Overprotecting children sends the message that they can't handle adversity, which undermines their confidence and growth."

One teacher shared a story of a parent who demanded daily progress updates – not because the child had additional needs, but simply because the parent believed constant monitoring was essential. Another teacher described a parent who wanted her child excused from PE because "running might overwhelm him". The child in question was perfectly healthy and played football every weekend.

Academic Integrity? Not Always

When it comes to academic integrity, parents can sometimes cross the line. A 2019 Chartered College of Teaching survey found that "teachers frequently encounter cases of parental interference in assignments". Anna, a history teacher, recalls a parent who rewrote her daughter's essay to the point that it sounded like a university thesis. "When I questioned it, the parent was unapologetic, saying, 'I was just helping her express herself better.'"

I've experienced it firsthand. A mother submitted an essay that was clearly written by someone with a degree-level grasp of English. When questioned, she explained, "I was just helping him express his ideas". Somewhere along the way, "help" had evolved into doing the entire assignment.

Amidst the chaos, there are still parents who approach these partnerships with genuine intention. They ask, "How can I support my child's learning?" They listen, collaborate, and respect the challenges of teaching. These rare interactions remind us of what's possible when parents and teachers work together.

Where Does This Leave Us?

The uncomfortable truth is that the education system isn't just strained by funding cuts, overcrowded classrooms and Ofsted pressures. It's also hindered by a growing disconnect between teachers and parents. Unless both sides recommit to mutual respect and accountability, it's the pupils who will pay the price.

Teachers are told to endure, to remain professional no matter the provocation. But the cracks are showing. Every confrontation, every unreasonable demand, chips away at the passion that brought us into teaching in the first place until we are left wondering if the job is worth all this aggravation.

It's time for a shift. For parents and teachers to rebuild trust, reframe expectations, and remember that at the heart of every interaction is a child relying on us to get it right.

CHAPTER 9

THE IN-CROWD: POWER, PRIVILEGE AND THE COST OF BIAS

In the world of teaching, where merit and dedication are supposed to define success, another invisible force holds immense sway: the power of influence. Teachers encourage the young people in our care to value equality and fairness, yet many do not embody these ideals themselves, choosing instead to pursue a more divisive approach in order to have an easier life. As such, the staffroom can sometimes appear more like a social club, where popularity breeds success and a "pecking-order" is clearly in operation. If you're in the in-crowd, life becomes a smoother ride. Mistakes are overlooked, promotions handed out with ease, and there's a clear pathway in your career progression. A protective bubble shields you from the relentless scrutiny that comes with teaching. But if you're outside the clique, the experience is harsher: constant surveillance, magnified missteps and often little to no support.

Take Nora, a colleague who played the politics of teaching like a seasoned pro. The SLT adored her for her charm, well-connected network and her ability to share just enough departmental gossip to remain indispensable. One year, Nora entered the wrong official A-level grades for her drama students — awarding low-ability students top grades and vice versa. It was an administrative disaster waiting to explode. Management discovered the error, but instead of addressing it transparently, they swept it under the rug. Students and parents were never informed, and there were no formal repercussions for Nora. "It's an honest mistake," they said. "These things happen." Had it been anyone else, it would likely have sparked investigations, parental complaints and even a formal warning.

Contrast this with Kieron, another colleague who dared to challenge the status quo. Kieron wasn't a bad teacher — in fact, he was a diligent professional and heavily involved with the union. But he made the mistake of being outspoken, questioning inconsistencies in school policies and calling out SLT decisions. For obvious reasons, management didn't like this. When Kieron forgot to upload a set of attendance records — a minor administrative slip-up — he wasn't given the benefit of the doubt. Meetings were called, his professionalism was questioned and he was dragged through a disciplinary process. For Kieron, the price of being on the wrong side of the SLT was heavy.

This bias doesn't just apply to classroom teachers. The higher up you go in the hierarchy, the more glaringly the in-crowd advantage reveals itself. Take the deputy head at one school I worked in. His temper was legendary — students and staff alike whispered about incidents where he had physically pushed students against walls during moments of anger. Parental complaints poured in, but they were systematically silenced. Meetings with parents were strategically managed to minimise fallout, and the deputy head remained untouchable. "He gets results" was the standard defence. Results mattered more than integrity, and loyalty more than accountability.

For those outside the circle, the rules are entirely different. A less-favoured teacher faced backlash simply for raising their voice to control a rowdy classroom. Complaints were logged, followed by formal observations and a series of "capability" meetings. The contrast was stark.

The in-crowd doesn't just protect its members; it propels them. Nora, despite her administrative blunders, climbed the ladder rapidly. Within three years, she was promoted to head of year, then assistant headteacher. Meanwhile, I witnessed senior colleagues, teachers with decades of experience, being overlooked for promotions. Their contributions weren't recognised, and their aspirations dismissed. "Not a good fit," they were told – a euphemism for "not one of us".

One particularly glaring example involved two head of year positions advertised internally. It was clear from the start who was being primed for the roles: two young teachers, both relatively new to the profession but well-connected to the headteacher. Meanwhile, a senior teacher who had been performing the role informally for years was offered the consolation prize of a deputy head of year position. She was crushed. Within months of these appointments, the headteacher was removed from their position for unrelated reasons, and both appointees began to struggle in their new roles. One stepped down after two months, leaving the senior teacher to be appointed to the position by the new headteacher. The senior teacher had to clean up the mess, taking on the role she should have had from the start.

The divide between the in-crowd and the outsiders isn't solely about professional favouritism; it can also be based on superficial judgements like a person's appearance, age or even assumptions derived from staffroom gossip. This inevitably breeds resentment, isolates talented teachers and fosters a toxic work environment. For those on the outside, the burden is immense. You witness it, despise it, and, as a teacher, you often find yourself working twice as hard for half the recognition, constantly under scrutiny. Meanwhile, others seem to advance effortlessly, leveraging their connections. This isn't to say that all teachers in the in-crowd lack merit – many are skilled and dedicated. However, the reduced scrutiny and greater freedom they enjoy often allows them to thrive, while others are left to struggle. Speaking up about this inequality is risky, as it can come across as bitterness, and the systemic nature of the issue makes it difficult to prove. Even colleagues who recognise the imbalance often remain silent, perhaps hoping they might one day join the privileged circle themselves.

The research confirms what many of us already know: favouritism in schools is real and pervasive. A study conducted by the Education Policy Institute found that personal relationships often play a more significant role in SLT appointments than actual qualifications or performance. The implications are dire; talented professionals are sidelined, while mediocrity – wrapped in a veneer of loyalty – thrives.

What's even more tragic is what happens when someone in the in-crowd falls out of favour. Their fall from grace is swift, brutal and often humiliating. I once worked in a school where a deputy head on an inflated annual salary of £150k (one of the perks of being in a relationship with the former headteacher) found himself in this very position. The new management wanted him out; he didn't fit their new vision, and the once overbearing and obnoxious leader suddenly became a champion of teachers against the SLT. He sought allies among those he had previously dismissed, navigating his new reality with desperation. It was a humiliating reminder of how fragile the in-crowd's protection truly is.

While much of the focus on in-crowd dynamics revolves around staff, the impact on students is arguably the most significant consequence. When a school's SLT prioritises personal loyalties over professional competence, it can lead to inconsistencies in teaching quality across the school. Favoured staff members may be shielded from scrutiny, allowing underperformance in classrooms to persist unchecked. Students in these classrooms may suffer from lower-quality teaching, limited engagement and missed opportunities for growth. Meanwhile, teachers outside the in-crowd, who may be more effective but face constant surveillance, often struggle to sustain the energy and morale required to provide a high-quality learning experience.

This creates a ripple effect: students see that accountability is selective, fostering a culture of unfairness and, in some cases, eroding their respect for authority. Ultimately, the in-crowd dynamic doesn't just damage staff morale – it compromises the very foundation of education, leaving students to bear the brunt of the SLT's bias.

PART 3

PERSONAL IMPACT – THE HUMAN COST

CHAPTER 10

COLLATERAL DAMAGE OF TEACHING

An unfortunate reality of the current teaching environment is that every action – every raised voice, missed email or small misstep – is scrutinised as if the educator is constantly on trial. Everyone is a judge; the students, parents, colleagues and SLT. In such a tense work setting, it is natural to feel anxious and constantly on-edge. The smallest glance can feel like an unspoken reminder that you're one mistake away from an "informal" meeting that could quickly escalate into a disciplinary hearing. But this isn't paranoia; this is the reality for thousands of teachers working in toxic schools all over the country.

And the unions we thought were our safety nets, they're supposed to protect us, right? At least, that's what we're told when we first enter the profession. But when the time comes, when accusations start flying and you're drowning in paperwork and desperate emails, the union's support often amounts to little more than a generic checklist. "Make sure you document everything," they'll say. But what exactly are we supposed to document, the growing sense that our headteacher is looking for any excuse to put us on a capability plan? The "support plan" that feels more like an eviction notice than actual assistance. Too often, we find ourselves abandoned, left to navigate a complex system that seems designed to catch us out, while the union quietly fades into the background.

It's no wonder that so many teachers don't fully understand their rights. We are so overwhelmed by lesson planning, grading and endless administrative tasks that we have little time to learn the policies that are being used against us. SLTs have a well-developed playbook of tactics designed to keep us in line, and unions, often stretched thin, are unable to offer meaningful protection. As a result, we become like lone soldiers in a war we didn't even know we were fighting, with policies weaponised to justify every misstep. "Struggling with behaviour management? Let's talk about a formal plan". "Your lesson plan didn't include the latest initiative mentioned in this morning's staff briefing? Time for a chat". That "chat" becomes a warning, and that warning quickly turns into a disciplinary file.

And when the pressure finally becomes too much, when every move you make is monitored and teaching feels like being on a reality TV show where the goal is simply not to be voted off, what happens when your mental health starts to unravel? Here's what happens: you find yourself in a doctor's office, clutching a fit note for stress. You start taking anti-depressants, going to therapy – anything to stay afloat. But for many, it doesn't stop there. You return to work, only to find that nothing has changed, even for those with recommendations for adjustments from an occupational health assessment. Another warning. Another "review" of your performance. Another step closer to the exit door.

And if you're "lucky"? You're quietly shown the door, pushed into early retirement or dismissed with a settlement that seems generous at first, until you realise it barely covers the bills for a couple of months. Then once you're out, there's the stigma. The inevitable question in every future job interview: "Why did you leave?" And let's be honest – teaching leaves scars that don't heal. Many leave the profession, but the trauma stays with them.

Still, people look at us and say, "You're lucky to have the summers off". If only they knew. Summers are our time to try to recover, to rebuild ourselves, to hope that maybe, just maybe, next year will be different. But deep down, we know the truth: next year will likely be the same. We tell ourselves that this time, the workload will ease. This time, the parents won't demand perfection if their child gets a grade 7 instead of a 9. This time, the SLT will step in to help when there's a fight in the corridor, rather than remaining in their offices and sending another email about "behaviour expectations".

We tell ourselves these things because the alternative is despair. We hold on to the hope that we might carve out some semblance of balance – some time to be with our families, to relax. But deep down, every teacher knows: the work doesn't stop at the end of the school day. Administrative tasks pile up, planning stretches into the evenings, and those 'quiet weekends' turn into marathon marking sessions. We're always preparing for Monday. The truth is, no matter how hard we work, it is never enough. The to-do list never ends.

And the worst part is, we are conditioned to believe that it's not okay to speak up. Teachers aren't supposed to admit they're struggling or acknowledge that sometimes the mental strain is too much. Even questioning the profession can feel like sacrilege, as though it means we're simply not cut out for the job. We start to believe that it's not the system that's broken, it's us. We look at colleagues who seem to handle everything just fine and feel even more like failures. What we don't see is that they too are probably struggling; maybe they're on their second anti-depressant prescription of the year or cried in their car that morning, sitting in the school car park, willing themselves to go inside and survive another day.

So, we suffer in silence. We put on a brave face, telling ourselves we can manage, even as our mental health deteriorates. And if we finally crack, we know what happens: the school will say it's "out of their hands". They'll "support" you all the way to a disciplinary meeting and then whisper to your colleagues that you simply couldn't handle the pressure.

We keep pushing through because that's what teachers do. We get up at dawn, drink our coffee just to function and pour everything we've got into our students – even if it means there's nothing left for ourselves or our families at the end of the day. And every once in a while, there's a student who says "thank you", a lesson that goes well or a spark of understanding in a student's eyes. Those moments keep us going. They're why we stay. Is that really worth it though? Is that really enough of a reason to stay, in the face of so many reasons to leave?

Teaching doesn't just drain you physically and mentally; it seeps into every corner of your personal life, leaving relationships hanging by a thread. It's a cruel irony – spending your days nurturing, mentoring and providing stability for other people's children, while your own family watches you slowly unravel from the sidelines.

Meet Ellie, an English teacher with nine years in the profession. On the surface, Ellie seems to have it all together – passionate about her job, dedicated to her students and always meeting her deadlines. But beneath the surface, Ellie is running on empty.

Teaching has infiltrated every part of her life, and the cracks are starting to show.

Ellie is a mother of two, married to a partner who isn't a teacher. While she spends her days nurturing other people's children, her own children miss out. Ellie recalls a moment when she had to miss her child's Nativity play because the headteacher didn't grant her leave request, stating that her focus needed to remain on her pupils and it would be "too disruptive to their learning" if she took the afternoon off. It's heartbreaking, but it's a reality many teachers face. Teachers miss birthdays, parents' evenings, and their own children's milestones, all in the name of providing care and stability for other children.

Ellie admits that her marriage has suffered as a result. "I come home, but I'm not really there," she says. "My husband doesn't understand why I can't just switch off. Why we can't have a date night on a Tuesday or even watch a film without me sneaking a glance at my emails. And if I'm not checking emails, I'm lying awake at night, worrying about tomorrow's lesson or that passive-aggressive comment from the SLT about my marking turnaround time, even though I've never missed a deadline".

For non-teaching spouses, it's often difficult to understand. The late nights, the Sunday dread, the endless meetings that bleed into evenings – it doesn't leave much room for spending quality time with partners. Teachers with non-teaching partners often hear, "It's just a job. Why are you bringing it home?" But teaching is never "just a job" and that's a hard concept for those with non-teaching careers to grasp. There is no "work-life balance" in teaching.

When Teaching Becomes a Third Wheel

Ellie's story isn't unique. A recent survey by Education Support revealed that 62% of teachers said their workload negatively impacts their relationships. The hours aren't just long, they're relentless. "My husband calls my job the 'third wheel in our marriage'," Ellie laughs, though the bitterness is clear. "He jokes about it, but I know it hurts him. I've missed anniversaries for parents' evenings. I've cancelled family plans to write reports. He's had to take our youngest to the park alone more times than I can count because I was buried in marking".

Teaching invades every part of your life, often leading to the unintended neglect of children and partners. For many, it results in broken marriages and resentful offspring.

The Cost of Giving Everything

Ellie recalls overhearing her daughter once say, "Mummy cares more about her students than us". It was a punch to the gut. "It's not that I don't care," Ellie says, "it's that I can't stop. The job consumes you, and you don't realise by how much until it's too late. Teaching is like a toxic relationship – it gaslights you into believing it's worth it, even when you're giving everything and receiving nothing in return".

The system isn't just flawed – it's abusive. It takes what you're willing to give, demands more, and leaves you with nothing but exhaustion and self-doubt. And even when you leave teaching, the scars remain. Teaching institutionalises you, training you to function under constant pressure, but only within the confines of the system. Once you're out, you're left questioning who you are without the chaos. The outside world feels alien, like you've been released from a cult without any deprogramming.

Teachers who leave often say they'll never fully recover. One Facebook commenter shared, "Even now, years after leaving, I still wake up from nightmares where I'm standing in front of a classroom, unsure of what I'm supposed to be teaching".

The Truth We Don't Talk About

We don't talk about how teaching fractures relationships. We don't talk about how it demands loyalty at the expense of our families. We don't talk about the guilt; missing your child's sports day because you had to run an after-school club or skipping your partner's promotion dinner because you had a pile of essays to mark.

And when you finally walk away, the guilt doesn't go away. You lie awake at night, wondering if you've failed – not just as a teacher, but as a parent, a partner and a person. The system breaks you, and the pieces don't always fit back together. But the system doesn't care. It doesn't care about your marriage, your mental health, or your children. It only cares about meeting targets and keeping Ofsted off its back.

And yet, despite everything, teachers continue to wake up, pour their coffee and return to the chaos. Why? Because somewhere in that madness, amid the shattered remnants of a broken system, there is still hope. Hope that maybe the sacrifices will mean something. That the next generation will be better for it.

CHAPTER 11

SHATTERED TRUST: A TEACHER'S ORDEAL

Teaching is often idealised as a profession of trust and mutual respect – a calling bound by the weighty responsibility of nurturing young minds. Yet, behind this noble façade lies a darker truth: one misinterpreted action or unfounded rumour can trigger a swift and unforgiving descent into a private hell.

In just one week, I encountered nine posts in a teaching Facebook group, each recounting a similar ordeal:

> "The worst week of my teaching career…I was accused of hitting a child and pulling their arm. The case was forwarded to LADO [the Local Authority Designated Officer]. Thankfully, investigations proved it was unsubstantiated and a false allegation."
>
> Anonymous Member 1

> "What a week. Advice, please. A child in my class made an official accusation about me – something that could have ended my career…"
>
> Anonymous Member 2

> "What is standard procedure for a student returning to school after admitting to making a false accusation against a member of staff?…Before the Easter half-term, a student made a false allegation against me. I was suspended for three days while an investigation took place. Fortunately, the student later confessed they had fabricated the whole thing."
>
> Anonymous Member 3

These are just fragments of a painful and deeply personal struggle that too many educators face – a struggle that often goes unspoken, let alone understood. Unless you've lived it, it's impossible to fully grasp the weight of these experiences.

When an accusation is made, it is not just a casual claim, it is a thunderous blow that can shatter a teacher's world. Years of hard work, dedication and a well-earned positive reputation are suddenly placed under a glaring, unforgiving spotlight. The familiar rhythm of the classroom gives way to the crushing isolation of suspicion, as every interaction and word is dissected, doubted and judged – often by people who have no insight into your side of the story.

The investigation process is a shadowy maze, a place where even if innocent, you feel perilously fragile. It strips teachers of their identity, reducing them to mere subjects of scrutiny. Dreams of career progression, the respect painstakingly earned over years, and even mental health teeter on the brink. And the harshest reality is that for many, the presumption of innocence is a luxury that disappears the moment an accusation is uttered.

One misinterpreted action, one false rumour, and the descent begins. It is a silent storm, leaving teachers battling not only to clear their name but also to piece together their shattered sense of self.

This chapter is not an easy one to write; it forces us to confront the darker truths of an otherwise noble profession. Yet, it is vital to lay bare these experiences; not just to highlight the vulnerability of educators, but to remind us all of the profound trust we place in this delicate and essential role.

In speaking with several teachers who endured false allegations, I found a common thread running through their stories: the profound and lasting impact these experiences had on their lives. Below is the account of one individual who shared his journey with me, offering a glimpse into the emotional toll and resilience required to navigate such a harrowing ordeal.

The Breakdown of Trust

Imagine a seasoned teacher in his mid-forties, a father of two, who has devoted over two decades to shaping young minds. His commitment and outspoken approach have made him well-known and respected within the school community. Yet, those same qualities have earned him the label of "problematic" from senior leadership over time. His forthright stance on issues others shy away from, and his challenging of the status quo, have not gone unnoticed. As the years go by, he's assigned the most challenging classes and told it's due to his "experience". But he senses the truth: these classes are less a compliment and more a burden – a target for failure.

Then, without warning, his world shatters. A student, notorious for disruptive behaviour, accuses him of rough handling – an allegation with no evidence, based solely on the student's word. Yet, that's enough. In the blink of an eye, his career veers off course. Senior leadership doesn't seek his account of the event; they see the accusation as a golden opportunity to finally get rid of him. His decades of service mean nothing. He's promptly suspended and marched off the premises with the cold justification that this is "for the safety of the children".

As he leaves the school grounds, everything is stripped away: his access to his students, colleagues and the community that once shaped his world. His entire professional network is severed, leaving him alone in the aftermath.

The Student's Lie and the System's Response

Behind the scenes, the story grows darker. The student who made the claim, despite knowing it was a lie, finds himself in too deep to back out. Admitting the truth now would mean facing severe consequences, possibly even expulsion. Encouraged by the attention and approval from certain classmates, he digs in deeper, fuelling the lie. In some circles, he's even seen as a hero – someone brave enough to take down a teacher who was "too strict" and "always gave detentions". He receives praise from peers, who admire the audacity of his story. And as it spreads, the lie grows, morphing from a minor accusation into tales of abuse and violence.

Meanwhile, the teacher sits at home, his mind in turmoil. He replays every classroom interaction, questioning every word and action. The words, "The truth will set you free" ring hollow. He knows this isn't about the truth. It's about evidence – or the lack thereof – turning the game into something rigged against him.

The investigation begins. Statements are taken, but to him, it feels like a tick-box exercise. The school has no stake in his well-being; they are a machine, focused only on reputation management. His years of service are cast aside in the desperate bid for institutional safety.

Gossip spreads like wildfire. Other students, parents and even staff whisper behind closed doors. Rumours reach social media, where the original accusation mutates into wilder stories. What started as a whisper of a grab now becomes tales of violence – chokeholds, knockout punches. And through it all, he is forced into silence, unable to defend himself publicly. His union, his supposed shield, offers little comfort; they are hard to reach, and when they do respond, their advice is simply to "wait it out". He realises he is not just alone; he has been abandoned.

The Emotional Toll

Weeks turn into months, and his life is put on indefinite hold. Many outside the profession fail to understand the weight of such allegations or the way investigations can stretch over half a year or more. These situations often escalate, involving the police, despite an absence of any substantive evidence. For those under scrutiny, the process is invasive and relentless.

As part of the investigation, he faces the real and terrifying prospect of having to leave his own home. The mere presence of children in his household triggers protocols that involve social services, with the implicit threat that his children could be removed if allegations are not disproven swiftly. It is a scenario that no parent or innocent professional should have to endure.

The police involvement adds an additional layer of fear and uncertainty. The formalities begin with an interview under caution at the station. His union has arranged for a lawyer to accompany him, but even with legal representation, the process is intimidating. Sitting in the stark, impersonal interview room, he feels exposed, as though his years of service and professionalism count for nothing.

The allegations are read out coldly, stripped of context, reduced to a series of claims he must now defend. Each statement is dissected with forensic precision, every response scrutinised for inconsistencies. The questions feel relentless, designed to probe, confuse and trip him up. How can he possibly recall every word spoken, every action taken, every fleeting decision made in the chaos of a busy classroom? They demand an explanation as to why a student would fabricate such accusations – as if he could read the mind of a teenager with their own agenda.

The lawyer offers reassurance and ensures that his rights are upheld, but it feels like a small comfort in a process that seems to presume guilt. The questioning ends, but the waiting is the most excruciating part. Days stretch into weeks, and then months. Every ring of the phone or knock at the door sends his heart racing, fearing the worst.

Sleepless nights, anxiety and depression become constants as his mental health deteriorates under the weight of isolation and uncertainty. His confidence is eroded, his professional identity shaken. The looming financial strain of a legal defence also hangs over him, even with the support of his union.

Finally, after what feels like an eternity, he is given a date: the case has been reviewed and the decision is "No Further Action" (NFA). Relief is immediate but bittersweet. Though the legal ordeal is over, the scars remain – his reputation tarnished, his mental health shattered and his trust in the systems meant to protect both staff and students irreparably damaged.

But the nightmare isn't over. With the police investigation concluded, the mandatory school disciplinary investigation looms ahead.

Possible Outcomes

The school's investigation, like the police's, seems to focus on procedural appearances rather than fairness or empathy. The possible outcomes are grim: a warning, dismissal or – if he's fortunate – complete exoneration. Even if cleared, the stigma of the accusation lingers. Among parents, students and even colleagues, he is likely to remain "the teacher who was accused".

Dismissal carries its own devastating consequences. A referral to the Teaching Regulation Agency (TRA) could lead to the ultimate punishment: the revocation of his teaching licence. This would not only end his career but render years of study, hard work and dedication meaningless. If the situation escalates to a tribunal, he would face a gruelling legal battle that could drag on for years, draining his savings and further eroding his mental health.

As the weeks stretch on, he begins to question everything that brought him here. Why didn't he challenge the decision to give him the toughest classes? Why did he push for change when it would have been easier to go with the flow? Why didn't he see the warning signs and take steps to protect himself? In the rare, quiet moments of reflection, he is haunted by the bitter truth: loyalty and dedication have made him a target in a system that too often treats its most committed staff as expendable.

The Aftermath: No Undo Button

When the school finally concludes its investigation, the truth emerges: the student fabricated the entire story. But the relief of vindication is muted. The damage has been done. The student faces no meaningful consequences. "At his age," the leadership team explains, "it wouldn't be appropriate to punish him".

For the teacher, however, the fallout is life-changing. His reputation is irreparably damaged. Students whisper about him in hallways, parents glance at him with suspicion and colleagues avoid him as if guilt lingers, even in innocence. His confidence is shattered, leaving him unsure whether he can ever return to the profession he once loved.

Even as he tries to move on, the ordeal leaves a scar. In education, where reputation is everything, rebuilding feels impossible. The trust he once placed in the system has been replaced by a stark realisation: he may have cleared his name, but he can never erase the impact of the accusation.

The Wider Impact

His suffering isn't unique. Studies reveal that up to 22% of teachers subjected to false allegations leave the profession altogether, unable to bear the mental strain. Others grapple with anxiety, PTSD and depression long after their cases conclude. The Association of Teachers and Lecturers (ATL) reports that many teachers never fully recover from such profound psychological impacts, leaving scars on their careers and lives.[v]

For this teacher, and countless others who have fallen into the abyss of allegations, the message is clear: in a system driven by procedure and protocol, loyalty and dedication are dispensable. Once the wheels are in motion, innocence is little more than a fragile hope. Even if exonerated, the scars remain – reputational damage, broken trust, and the lingering fear that it could happen again. And when it's all over, all that's left is survival; piecing together what remains of a career that once felt meaningful but now feels precarious at best.

Compounding the Nightmare

What makes this reality even harder to accept is the grim truth that many students are increasingly adept at weaponising school policies to their advantage. False accusations against teachers are made with little regard for the consequences, and even when the lies are exposed, the repercussions for the students are often negligible – typically a token suspension, or worse, excused with vague references to "family issues" or "emotional challenges".

Meanwhile, teachers are left to bear the full weight of these accusations. This imbalance in accountability fosters a toxic culture, where manipulation thrives, trust is eroded, and dedicated educators are driven out. The result is a system that fiercely protects its policies but fails the very people who uphold them.

A Potential Solution

To address this toxic culture of false accusations and teacher isolation, schools must implement a zero-tolerance policy for false claims, with clear, enforceable consequences for students who make them. If an accusation is proven false, the student should face serious repercussions – formal disciplinary action, suspension, or even referral to external support services if necessary.

At the same time, schools must provide immediate, comprehensive support to teachers under investigation. Legal representation, counselling and peer advocacy should be standard practices, not optional ones. Teachers need unions and leadership teams that actively fight for their rights – not ones that leave them struggling in the face of bureaucracy.

Moreover, schools must cultivate a culture of transparency, where teachers can defend themselves openly without fear of reputational damage. Protecting teachers from baseless accusations should be seen as just as critical as safeguarding students from harm.

Moving Forward

The changes required go beyond mere policy adjustments; they demand a fundamental shift in how schools balance accountability with fairness. Schools must foster a culture of mutual respect, where teachers are viewed as valuable professionals, deserving of the same safeguarding and support that students receive. Without this shift, the cycle will continue – good teachers will be driven out, trust between staff and students will erode, and a system that lacks compassion and integrity will persist.

The stakes couldn't be higher. Every teacher lost to these injustices is not only a personal tragedy but a loss to the entire education system. If we fail to address this, we risk more than just damaged careers – we risk the very future of education itself.

CHAPTER 12

THE MENTAL HEALTH TOLL OF TEACHING

> "I love teaching, but my mental health was suffering. At the ripe old age of 55, I've finally learned to value my own well-being."
>
> Helen

> "I've developed mental health issues over the course of this year. Some of it is related to home and finances, but a significant amount comes from school – office politics and shameless favouritism."
>
> Anonymous

> "My mental health is worse than ever. I've been diagnosed with severe burnout and anxiety, feeling hopeless and trapped."
>
> Esme

These were just three posts I recently read in an online teacher forum.[vi] They are far from unique. They reflect a growing crisis within the profession, where mental health is being ground down by unrelenting pressure. Teaching is killing us. This isn't hyperbole – it's a stark reality, one that's increasingly backed by data.

The Relentless Toll

In recent years, the requirement for cover teachers in schools has significantly increased, to the point where on any given day, the list of lessons needing cover will be substantial. Subsequently, the scramble to find supply teachers is constant. It's not due to flu season, and it's not just bad luck. Those absences aren't just colds or coughs; they're breakdowns.

According to the Teacher Wellbeing Index, 78% of school staff experienced mental health issues due to their work in the past year. Over 50% are actively considering leaving the profession. This isn't a case of mild stress; it's a systemic mental health crisis.[vii]

In the last academic year alone, 2.5 million school days were lost to teacher absences, many of them related to stress, anxiety, and burnout (*The Telegraph*, 2023). That's more than 14,000 teachers missing every single day. These aren't just numbers, they're alarm bells. Each absence represents a professional pushed to their breaking point.

Behind the Data: Real Lives Breaking

Behind every empty classroom or frantic supply teacher briefing, there's a colleague who has quietly cracked. Some call in sick. Others take that final, desperate step out of the door and never come back. And those still standing? Many are holding on by a thread.

I'll never forget the day I warned a former student of mine – now training to be a teacher – that the job would test her in ways she couldn't imagine. "I'm ready," she said with optimism. She sailed through her PGCE and started as an NQT. Just six months in, she texted me: "I can't do this anymore. I thought teaching was about helping kids. But it's just constant pressure. I feel like I'm drowning."

Then there was Mr Norris, the headteacher who once commanded respect with a single glance. Over time, I watched him unravel under the weight of it all. In a tense staff meeting, he screamed, "Leave if you don't want to be here!" Weeks later, he took a leave of absence over Christmas, citing "personal reasons". When he returned, he was a shadow of his former self. The breaking point came when he nearly got into a physical fight with a parent. By summer, he was gone, looking for work elsewhere.

These anecdotes are the reality of teaching today.

Why Are We Breaking?

The reasons are painfully clear and overwhelmingly damning:

1. **The Crushing Workload**

    Teachers work an average of **50–60 hours a week**, with only **30%** of that time spent teaching. The remaining hours are swallowed by administrative tasks, behaviour reports, lesson planning, marking, meetings, extra-curricular activities and parental contact (*Education Policy Institute, 2022*). Many of us work into the night and through weekends, sacrificing sleep, family time and health just to stay afloat.

2. **Toxic Accountability**

   Ofsted inspections hang over every school like a guillotine. Often the threat of a looming inspection can prompt "mock inspections" and department "deep dives", conducted by SLTs or external consultants who are paid to put staff through their paces. These practice runs and the constant scrutiny that ensues creates a toxic culture of pressure and mountains of additional paperwork which inevitably does more harm than good. By the time Ofsted actually does visit, staff are burned out, miserable and have lost any desire to put on the necessary show.

3. **Classroom Chaos**

   Poor behaviour within the student body is spiralling out of control. **70% of teachers** report being verbally or physically abused by students (*Scottish Sun, 2024*). Dealing with constant disruption drains not just your time, but your emotional reserves.

4. **No Value Added**

   Teachers are increasingly feeling undervalued both in terms of financial recompense and the status of the profession in wider society. Stagnant salaries, limited career progression and a complete lack of work-life balance mean that we are often left feeling like the poor relation in comparison to our peers. University reunions are galling – seeing how your contemporaries (with the same or fewer qualifications) have soared in their chosen fields and have amassed a sizeable income with great employment benefits can leave most teachers feeling bitter and questioning their choices. Why do we do this again? That feeling multiplies when we are told that we have "cushy" jobs and should "stop complaining" by politicians and parents, who do not want to accommodate their own children when school staff take the difficult decision to strike over pay and conditions. We are torn to shreds in the media and made to feel like villains for simply asking for better. Is it any wonder then, that we are tired of being undervalued and are dreaming of getting out.

The following is a story that a colleague has given me permission to share.

A Teacher's Story

It wasn't one moment that broke me – it was a thousand little ones. Each email, each reprimand, each failed attempt to reach a student chipped away at me until there was nothing left.

My daughter had just been born. Beautiful, perfect, and utterly dependent on me. Most nights, I was running on two hours of sleep, juggling bottles and nappies before dawn, and then heading into the most draining environment imaginable: a chaotic secondary school in central London.

The school was a pressure cooker. Low-ability students had been given sky-high target grades, and we were expected to make miracles happen. Many of my Year 11s struggled to read at a primary school level, yet their GCSE target grades were 7s. "It's aspirational," my line manager said when I raised concerns. "You just need to push harder."

Pushing harder meant hours of after-school interventions and weekend revision sessions. It meant marking mock exams in the early hours for students who barely turned up to lessons. And it all went unnoticed.

The emails were relentless. "Update your data tracker." "Log every behaviour incident." "Why isn't Student X on track for their target grade?" My inbox was a constant reminder that nothing I did was ever enough.

My Year 10s were unmanageable. Phones out, eating in class, outright defiance. I'd walk into the room and be met with blank stares or outright laughter. "Dickhead," one boy muttered during a lesson. Another threw a tennis ball at a student while I was explaining the coursework. Reporting incidents to management was pointless – they either ignored the issues or turned them back on me. "What are you doing to engage them?" they'd ask, as if the problem was my fault.

The meetings after school were the worst. Endless, pointless sessions about data or behaviour policies that didn't work. Every so often, a senior leader would drop a sarcastic comment: "It's about mindset. Some of you need to work smarter, not harder." We all knew what it meant: you're not doing enough.

By the time I got home, I barely had time to see my wife or daughter before collapsing into bed. But sleep didn't come. My mind raced with everything I hadn't done. Had I updated the intervention spreadsheet? Was my seating plan up to date? Would the head call me out in the next staff meeting?

The Breakdown

It came on a Wednesday. My Year 9s had been impossible all week, and I was already on edge. That morning, a fight broke out over a pen. By the time I separated them, one boy was shouting in my face, calling me names I won't repeat. The rest of the class laughed.

I reported it to my line manager. Her response? "You need to build a stronger rapport. You can't expect respect if you don't earn it."

Something inside me snapped. I nodded, walked out of her office, and locked myself in the staff toilets. The fluorescent lights flickered above me. I could hear the muffled chaos of the corridor, but it felt a world away. My breathing was shallow, my hands clammy. *"I can't do this anymore,"* I whispered to myself, over and over, like a mantra I didn't believe.

I sat there shaking, my chest tight, my head spinning, struggling to breathe. I couldn't go back into the classroom. I couldn't go home. I felt trapped. I realised that I was having a panic attack. Luckily a colleague came to my aid and helped to calm me down, but for a moment there, I really thought that I might die in that bathroom under those flickering fluorescent lights.

That evening, my wife found me sitting in the kitchen, staring blankly at my laptop. "You're done," she said softly. "You can't keep doing this."

The End of the Line

The next morning, I handed in my resignation. The headteacher tried to talk me around, more concerned with how the students would cope than with my well-being. I walked out of that office with nothing left – no energy, no confidence, no sense of self. Teaching had drained it all.

That was six months ago. I'm still recovering. The sleepless nights have eased, but the memories linger. I think about the students I couldn't help, the colleagues I left behind and the system that chews up and spits out people like me.

Teaching didn't just exhaust me, it destroyed me and it will continue to break others unless something changes.

Teachers are burning out and breaking down. If we don't prioritise mental health and overhaul this broken system, the cost won't just be individual careers – it will be the collective futures of generations of children to come. Mental health matters, and without it, the education system cannot survive.

CHAPTER 13

THE SALARY SQUEEZE

How can I write a book with "survive" in the title and not address the elephant in the room. Pay. It's gut-wrenching to think that the so-called backbone of society is crumbling under financial strain. Imagine this: shaping the minds of future generations by day, then having to clock in for a night shift at Tesco or racing against the clock to deliver Uber Eats every evening whilst their own fridges remain empty due to lack of time to visit a food bank.

The cruel irony here is that if you ask most teachers why they joined the profession, they'll say, "It's not about the money, it's about the kids." Admirable, yes. But also hopelessly idealistic. Whilst they're busy pouring their souls into their students, the cost of living relentlessly keeps their bank accounts in the red – and British Gas isn't going to give them a pass just because they delivered an inspiring science lesson that morning.

Too many teachers undervalue themselves, prioritising the school's budget over their own financial security. They dodge conversations about pay like they're avoiding a poorly planned INSET day, all while silently bearing the brunt of stagnant wages. Meanwhile, money is there – just not where it should be.

According to a recent Guardian article, more than 200 academy heads in England are now earning over £150,000 a year, with some salaries reaching £330,000. That number has doubled in just five years. These are executive leaders at the top of multi-academy trusts – some of which oversee schools that are under-resourced, short-staffed and reliant on dedicated teachers working themselves into the ground. Executive heads aren't afraid to take home six-figure salaries, so you should not be scared to ask for a fair one.viii

Here's the hard truth: it's time to stop fearing the "money talk" and start demanding the pay you deserve.

The Salary Scale Illusion

In the UK, teacher pay is predominantly structured in a scale system, with M1–M6 making up the Main Pay Scale and the increasingly elusive UPS1–UPS3 (Upper Pay Scale) levels held up as the pinnacle of achievement. In theory, progression to UPS is based on experience, excellence and meeting professional targets. In practice, it's a bureaucratic maze. Many schools weaponise the system, attaching arbitrary goals to pay increases and blurring the lines between experience-based progression and responsibilities tied to TLRs. It's no wonder teachers feel like they're navigating a rigged game.

Meet Samantha, teacher of maths and a single parent with no family support. She earns £45,000 per year on the M5 pay scale under the outer London band (2024 rate). On paper, this sounds like a comfortable salary – until you look closer.

After deductions for income tax (20%), National Insurance (12%), and student loan repayments (9% on earnings over £27,295), Samantha's take-home pay shrinks to £2,725 per month. This is the money she has to cover rent, bills, groceries, childcare and everything else, in one of the most expensive regions in the country. She has already been forced to opt out of the TPS (Teacher Pension Scheme) in order to avoid a further 8.6% monthly deduction.

With no partner or family support to share the load, Samantha faces every financial challenge alone. And when you break it down, that £2,725 feels more like a cruel joke than a salary.

Bills That Crush You

Here's what Samantha's monthly budget looks like:

- **Accommodation**: £1,800 to cover rent, service charge and council tax for a small two-bedroom flat in Zone 5. Living closer to work isn't even an option. The market is brutal, and a single parent like Samantha doesn't have the luxury of house shares.
- **Utilities**: £250 currently, but this may increase in the near future because energy companies are squeezing every penny from families already on the edge and the water companies are now getting in on the act too.
- **Groceries**: £400 for herself and her 8-year-old son, Leo. This covers basics – no treats, no luxuries, no brand names.

Just on these essentials, Samantha is already spending £2,450, leaving her with just £275 to cover everything else.

Childcare: The Hidden Cost of Being a Teacher

Leo's school day doesn't align with Samantha's teaching hours, so she has to pay for after-school care. At £300 per month, it's non-negotiable if she wants to keep her job. That leaves her £25 in debt before even considering travel, clothing or unexpected costs.

But Samantha's costs don't end there. School trips for Leo come in at £10–£20 each, and after-school activities, like football or swimming, cost £50–£100 per term. These aren't luxuries – they're the basics of childhood. Yet for Samantha, they feel like indulgences she can't afford.

The Debt That Never Goes Away

When Samantha's car broke down last month, the £870 repair cost went straight onto her credit card. She's still paying off a £700 boiler repair from last winter, with interest piling on each month. The student loan deduction on her pay slip is another bitter pill – £132 per month for a debt she's barely making a dent in, thanks to interest rates of 7.3% (March 2024).

Her credit card balance grows, and she knows she's trapped in a cycle. Any unexpected expense tips her deeper into debt. Even a minor dental emergency or Leo needing new school shoes feels like a financial disaster waiting to happen.

Running on Empty

Samantha skips meals to make sure Leo eats. She turns off the heating and layers up in blankets, praying for warmer weather to ease the bills. Her fridge is often empty by the end of the month, with food banks creeping into the back of her mind as an option she never thought she'd need.

She hasn't bought herself new clothes in three years and a friend cuts her hair to avoid salon costs. As for socialising, that's a luxury Samantha gave up long ago. Nights out with friends have been replaced with marking, lesson planning and the relentless anxiety of how she'll make it through another month.

The Brutality of Teaching – Unpaid Overtime

Samantha's job doesn't end when the bell rings. Evenings are consumed with unpaid overtime: marking, lesson planning and attending endless meetings. She runs after-school revision sessions and lunchtime clubs because the school doesn't have enough staff to cover them. None of this is compensated.

In the past year, Samantha has spent £200 of her own money on classroom supplies: pens, art materials and even snacks for students who turn up hungry. It's the unspoken tax of teaching in a system that underfunds both its schools and its students.

Meanwhile, her school proudly invests in "staff well-being initiatives". Think motivational posters and yoga sessions no one has time to attend. If irony paid the bills, Samantha could finally breathe.

The Cost of a Broken System

According to the National Education Union, 12% of teachers have had to rely on food banks, and for single parents, the figure is even higher. Teachers like Samantha are not thriving – they're barely surviving.

Yet her school always seems to find money for other priorities: a £10,000 leadership conference or a new "Head of Student Engagement" position with a six-figure salary. When Samantha asks to move up the pay scale, she's met with a refusal due to "budget constraints". She could threaten to leave as leverage, but the very real threat of being replaced by a cheaper alternative (think an ECT on M1) if they call her bluff, prevents her from doing so.

The Negative Impact on Leo

Samantha hides her struggles from Leo, but the cracks are showing. He's already noticed the things they can't afford – school trips, birthday parties, new clothes – and it's starting to affect him.

Last Christmas, Samantha borrowed money to buy Leo a second-hand PlayStation from Facebook Marketplace. He didn't complain, but she saw the disappointment in his eyes when his friends talked about getting the newest version.

It shouldn't be this way. Not for a child whose parent works all hours and earns an annual salary of £45,000.

The Brutal Truth

Samantha's story lays bare the harsh reality faced by countless teachers across the UK. A profession lauded as 'noble' is crumbling under financial strain and systemic neglect. Despite her seemingly comfortable salary, Samantha is barely surviving – juggling crippling bills, unpaid overtime and the relentless pressures of single parenthood, all while delivering excellence in her classroom.

Her sacrifices go unnoticed in a system that prioritises budget cuts over retaining experienced staff, with many schools now opting to replace high-performing teachers like her with cheaper, less experienced (even unqualified) alternatives.

This is the brutal truth: teaching doesn't just demand dedication, it extracts everything, leaving teachers like Samantha financially and emotionally drained. Until pay, support and respect match the weight of their responsibilities, the education system will continue to bleed its most valuable assets dry, threatening all of our futures.

PART 4

TOXIC WORK ENVIRONMENTS – CULTURE AND LEADERSHIP

CHAPTER 14

WHEN LEADERSHIP FAILS

In any industry, teamwork is vital and a good manager should be the linchpin of a successful team. But in many schools, the opposite is true – poor management tears their staff apart. When incompetent individuals step into leadership roles, the focus shifts from team cohesion to power struggles, creating a toxic environment where egos overshadow the educational vision. For those in the trenches, this creates a daily nightmare that erodes morale, crushes ambition and ultimately drives teachers out of the profession.

During my career in education, I've experienced both ends of the leadership spectrum. On rare occasions, I've had the privilege of working under leaders who uplifted their teams. These individuals understood that leadership wasn't about asserting power but about enabling others to succeed. They knew how to provide constructive feedback, foster collaboration and create a culture of respect and growth. Under their guidance, you felt seen, heard and valued. They made you believe in the profession, even during its most challenging moments.

But then there are the power-hungry managers, the ones who crave authority but lack the competence to wield it responsibly. I once worked under a deputy head who seemed more interested in asserting dominance than in creating a positive working environment. His leadership style was a toxic mix of micromanagement and intimidation. Feedback sessions felt like public executions, where teachers were forced to justify every decision while he tore apart their efforts. Meetings weren't spaces for collaboration, they were arenas for his unchecked ego. His presence made you dread meeting days and his impact lingered long after you left his office.

A Case Study in Incompetence

When I stepped down from middle management and joined a new school, I hoped for a fresh start. Instead, I found myself working under a head of department so ill-prepared it was almost comical – until it wasn't. He lacked even the most basic understanding of educational frameworks. Key concepts like differentiation and SEND support were foreign languages to him. His plans for the department were either non-existent or cobbled together haphazardly, leaving the team directionless and demoralised.

This wasn't just incompetence, it was active negligence. When faced with challenges, he would fabricate data, pass blame onto his team and dodge accountability. His lack of leadership meant staff were unsupported, students fell through the cracks and the department's performance suffered. Complaints from parents and staff piled up, but the SLT turned a blind eye, unwilling to address the root of the problem and acknowledge their poor decision in appointing him.

Some of the most egregious examples of his ineptitude came during lesson observations. His feedback was vague at best, completely unhelpful at worst. When he failed his own observation by management, there was no follow-up, no intervention – just silence from senior leadership. For six months, the department remained in disarray. When he finally left under the guise of "work-related stress", brought on by one faux pas too many for the SLT, the collective relief amongst staff was palpable.

The Managerial Archetypes

Every school seems to accommodate the same predictable cast of managerial archetypes, each shaping the culture, morale and effectiveness of their teams in profoundly different ways. These leadership styles often feel like they've been plucked from a manual on organisational dysfunction, and their impact ripples far beyond the staffroom walls.

- **The Autocrat**: Commanding absolute authority, this leader makes decisions as if they were divine decrees, leaving no room for discussion or collaboration. The result? A stifling atmosphere thick with resentment, where sparks of creativity and innovation are rapidly extinguished.

- **The Incompetent One**: An individual so glaringly unsuited for leadership that their every decision leaves chaos in its wake. Staff are left scrambling to clean up after them, wasting energy that should be spent on actual teaching and learning.

- **The Micromanager**: Choking autonomy at every opportunity, they dictate everything from the font on a Powerpoint presentation to the length and format of starter activities. Their overreach creates a stifling environment devoid of trust and personal responsibility.

- **The Narcissist**: Their leadership revolves entirely around their own image. Staff well-being and student outcomes take a backseat to their obsessive need for approval from headteachers, governors or Ofsted. Often, they double as the **Bully**, ruling through fear and intimidation, and creating a fractured and anxious workplace.

- **The Indecisive One**: Paralysed by the weight of their role, this leader delays critical decisions endlessly, leaving staff adrift in uncertainty. Whether it's signing off timetables or enacting much-needed changes, their hesitance breeds inefficiency and frustration.

- **The Good Manager**: Rare and inspiring, this leader fosters collaboration, energises their teams, and unites everyone under a shared vision. Yet, even their leadership can feel precarious in the face of systemic pressures and the toxicity of their peers. As much as they uplift those around them, you can't help but wonder: how long can they endure?

What is most amusing about many of these managers is their chameleon-like ability to adapt their behaviour, depending on who is in the room and what they need from you. I've seen the most narcissistic members of an SLT suddenly become thoughtful and considerate when they require my support or need an ally in a situation. Their ability to manipulate the situation to their advantage shows just how deeply entrenched the dysfunction can be.

The Consequences of Poor Leadership

Poor leadership is a corrosive force that erodes the very foundation of a school. It turns educational environments into spaces of fear and resentment, where teachers feel silenced, unsupported and undervalued. Instead of focusing on what truly matters – teaching and learning – staff are mired in office politics, forced to compensate for managerial failings and exhausted from trying to keep the ship afloat.

The statistics are sobering: according to a survey carried out by TES, nearly half of UK teachers cite poor management as a key reason for leaving the profession. When leadership prioritises personal egos over effective team building, the fallout is devastating – staff burnout and plummeting retention rates, with a revolving door of talent that inevitably weakens the school's provision.

A Call for Change

The time for excuses is over. Schools must redefine leadership – not as a position of control, but as one of service. True leaders should act as mentors, advocates and facilitators, supporting their teams rather than obstructing them. The current culture of box-ticking and target-chasing must be replaced by one that values relationships and fosters growth.

Poor management can no longer be excused as the by-product of "stressful circumstances" or "tight budgets". If a leader cannot effectively support their team, they have no place being in that role. The stakes are too high. When leadership fails, it's not just the staff who suffer – it's the students, the community and the future of education itself.

This isn't just a call to action; it's a demand for accountability. When schools cultivate leaders who truly lead, who serve rather than dominate, everyone benefits. The ripple effects can transform not just classrooms, but lives.

CHAPTER

15

NO EXCUSES, NO ESCAPE

The previous chapter discussed the variety of poor leaders that plague school corridors, so it might feel superfluous to spend another chapter exploring the same topic. If you will indulge me though, I feel that the individual I am about to introduce you to deserves a chapter of their own, if only due to the very real impact that they had on my life.

Let me introduce you to an old colleague – a former SLT "warrior" who lived by the motto, "No excuses". He wore it like a badge of honour, strutting through the halls with an air of disdain, convinced that anyone who didn't thrive in the system simply wasn't cut out for it. To him, teaching was a battleground, a place for the strong to rise and the weak to fall. He commanded respect through fear, the same way you might fear a live wire dangling from the ceiling.

In his world, SLT wasn't just a leadership team; it was a "Secret Legion of Titans", there to weed out the faint-hearted and train the "elite". Teaching, according to him, was like SAS training – just with more sarcasm and fewer shouty drills. If you're struggling, well, it's your fault. "Teaching's a proving ground," he'd say, "the strong thrive, the weak whinge". To him, real teachers were the ones who could breeze through 14-hour days, unaffected by surprise Ofsted inspections or mountains of paperwork. "If you want an easy life," he'd laugh, "try working at a garden centre".

Ofsted: The Holy Grail of Accountability

Now, Ofsted. For most teachers, an Ofsted inspection is like walking into a firing squad armed with nothing but a notebook and dry markers. But for him? It was practically a national holiday. The man adored Ofsted. He believed they were the "holy grail of accountability". "Ofsted's not the enemy," he'd scoff, "they're here to make sure you're doing your job". If you dared mention that Ofsted stress might contribute to teachers' mental health crises, he'd cackle, "Oh please, that's called having a job!" To him, the fact that the system pushed teachers to the edge was just proof of natural selection – only the tough survive.

Unions: "Meddlers"

And then there were the unions. While most of us clung to our unions as a last line of defence against the relentless workload and absurd expectations, he saw them as "meddlers". "Half the school day wasted on union meetings," he'd complain. To him, unions were as useful as a chocolate teapot. He believed that if teachers managed their time properly, they wouldn't need "handholding" from a union. Teachers demanding pay rises? Outlandish! Teachers using food banks? He'd mutter something about "poor life choices" and quickly move on.

Burnout: A Natural Part of the Job?

Then came burnout. He dismissed it as just part of the job. Once, I mentioned that 40% of UK teachers consider leaving the profession within their first five years due to stress. He rolled his eyes and sneered, "Every industry has its casualties. Burnout? Try working in A&E". To him, teaching was an endurance event, designed to filter out the "weak". As for the thousands of teachers who left last year, they just couldn't "hack it". "The strong keep going, the weak leave," he'd say. He even took aim at teacher support groups online, calling them "whinge clubs". According to him, if you were a "real" teacher, pressure didn't break you – it polished you into a diamond. "Can't handle it?" he'd smirk, "Time for a career change".

The Irony of It All

Here's the twist, though. For all his talk of endurance and "no excuses," this titan of resilience eventually found himself on the receiving end of an SLT investigation. One too many staff complaints, a whisper of scandal here, a hint of misconduct there – suddenly the "strongest of the strong" was in the hot seat. The man who had preached about being untouchable, who had sneered at those who couldn't keep up, was now facing disciplinary action. His beloved "no excuses" mantra didn't hold up quite so well when the tables turned.

After a few months of tension, secret meetings, and closed-door "feedback sessions" that felt more like police interrogations, he slinked away with a settlement and a quiet exit.

From Enforcer to Casualty

In the end, the very system he had worshipped – the merciless, relentless machine – had chewed him up and spat him out. Once the untouchable enforcer of policies, wielding power with an iron fist, had become just another casualty of the institution he had so fervently upheld. Stripped of his authority, he walked out, a shadow of the person he once was.

The irony was unbelievable. Did he now understand the damage caused by the system? Could he finally see the careers derailed, the morale destroyed by the very rules he had so passionately enforced?

When I spoke to him again, his perspective had shifted dramatically. The confidence and self-righteousness was gone. In its place was quiet bitterness. He spoke of betrayal – not from the staff he once viewed as beneath him, but from those he had once counted as allies. The colleagues who smiled in meetings, nodding in agreement, were the same ones who had quietly undermined him at every turn. The school that claimed to value transparency and open communication was a façade, a place where backdoor politics and whispered alliances dictated survival. His downfall wasn't just a result of his own actions but of the toxic culture he had perpetuated.

For the first time, he admitted seeing the cracks in the system. But by then, the damage – both to him and the institution – had already been done.

CHAPTER 16

CONFRONTING SEXUAL HARASSMENT

I once believed that the classroom should be a sanctuary – a place where knowledge is shared, futures are built, and respect is the cornerstone. But for far too many teachers, particularly women, it is the complete opposite. These aren't the stories shared in training seminars or staff meetings; they're the ones whispered in terror, muted behind closed doors or swallowed down with bitter silence. Stories of groping hands, predatory stares, and words that cut like knives. Stories of trust shattered and safety abandoned, all under the watch of a system that promises protection but delivers betrayal.

Teaching is about more than just imparting knowledge. It's a constant balancing act between authority and compassion, patience and discipline, inspiration and practicality. But what happens when that balance is shattered, when the trust and safety that underpin our classrooms are eroded by actions that defy comprehension?

It starts small. A comment muttered under a student's breath – disrespectful, but easy to ignore. Then, a lingering look, a snicker, a gesture. You tell yourself it's nothing. You convince yourself you're imagining things. But the boundaries begin to blur. The comments escalate, their meaning unmistakable: "She's fit, I'll do her"; "Hey Miss, age is just a number". A hand brushes where it shouldn't. A student blocks your path. Students openly watch pornography on their phones during lunch. And before you know it, you're caught in a nightmare you never prepared for – a nightmare where you're the target, the victim, and the one expected to fix it all.

In an article titled "Very Intimidating: Teachers on Sexual Harassment by Pupils", published in *The Guardian*, journalist Sally Weale sheds light on a troubling reality within schools.[ix] Her words are both eye-opening and deeply unsettling, exposing an issue that many would prefer to ignore. For countless female teachers, this is not some distant or hypothetical concern – it is a lived experience. It's an insidious reality that thrives in silence, where speaking out feels like a betrayal of the very profession we hold dear. Yet, remaining silent comes at a cost, allowing this unspoken issue to fester in the shadows.

Just before completing this book, I came across a post on the aforementioned Facebook group that left me shaken to my core. A fellow teacher, working in an SEN school, laid her pain bare for colleagues to see. Her words were raw and heart-wrenching, a wound opened wide for anyone brave enough to look. It forced me to rewrite this chapter, struggling to hold back my anger.

"Hi all. I was recently sexually assaulted by a pupil at my school. (SEN school) Where do I even go from here? What should I expect to happen? I don't know if there's any situation, I would be happy with. I've notified my union, just awaiting a response. Sat here on a Saturday night, absolutely dreading going back on Monday... It started with up-skirting and exposing me to other pupils, and sexual touching of my chest. Now it has led to something much worse. I've reported all of these incidents to SLT/DSL, and they've told me to continue to use visuals to discourage this. My school does not suspend children, so I know nothing happened. I'm not even sure if their parents have been informed yet in my absence..."[x]

Her story haunted me – not just the details of what happened, but the resignation in her tone. It was the knowledge that no matter how loudly she screamed for help, the system was designed to block out the sound.

I've seen this same resignation etched on the faces of other female colleagues – teachers who flinch when certain students enter the room, who break down in the staffroom after yet another incident, who go home carrying bruises no one can see.

The true horror doesn't just lie in the actions of a few troubled students; it lies in the systemic failures that allow these behaviours to persist. Policies are written to protect, but in practice, they are riddled with loopholes. Senior leaders hesitate to act, fearing the reputational damage that might come with suspending or expelling a student. Teachers are advised to "de-escalate", "use strategies" or "build rapport". The real issue here is that, despite these well-meaning directives, no real action is taken to address the problem at its core.

What They're Really Saying is: Endure It

I once worked with a colleague who reported being groped by a student. The response from leadership was, "He comes from a difficult home. You need to show him kindness". When she pushed back, challenging the lack of support, they turned the issue back on her, questioning her professionalism as though her trauma was a reflection of her inadequacy rather than the student's behaviour.

The message was clear: Protect the school's reputation at all costs. Protect the student's future, even if it means sacrificing the teacher's safety.

It's not just teachers who are victims of unwanted sexual advances in schools either. A report by the National Education Union (NEU) revealed that over a third (37%) of female students in co-educational schools have personally experienced some form of sexual harassment at school. Nearly a quarter (24%) reported being subjected to unwanted physical touching of a sexual nature while at school.[xi]

The same report also found that nearly one in three (32%) teachers in co-educational secondary schools witness sexual harassment in their school at least once a week, with 6% observing such incidents daily. Clearly this is a serious issue which urgently needs addressing – so why is no-one openly talking about this and nothing being done?

The impact of these incidents doesn't end when the school bell rings. They follow you home, invade your thoughts, disrupt your sleep, and slowly erode your sense of self. You jump at shadows. You flinch when someone brushes past you in a crowded room. You question your worth, your strength, and your ability to continue in a profession you once loved.

Some teachers leave, their passion extinguished. Others stay, each day a battle between their dedication to their students and the fear that looms like a spectre. All carry scars, visible or not.

The Silence Must End

The silence cannot continue. The whispered stories of terror, betrayal and survival in the staffroom must erupt into a collective outcry for change. Schools must implement and enforce zero-tolerance policies for harassment and assault, with real consequences – not hollow platitudes or flimsy procedures that shift the burden onto the victims. Leadership must wake up to their moral and legal obligation to prioritise the safety of their staff just as much as their students.

For female teachers, who already bear the added weight of navigating a world that so often trivialises their pain, specific protections must be in place. This means mandatory training on recognising and responding to inappropriate behaviour, robust reporting systems that don't falter under bureaucracy, and tangible support mechanisms that offer more than sympathetic nods or empty reassurances.

Under Section 44 of the Employment Rights Act 1996 and Section 26 of the Equality Act 2010,[xii] teachers have the legal right to refuse to work in conditions that pose a serious and imminent danger to their health or safety. This right must be wielded as a weapon against institutions that fail to act – a line drawn in the sand against those who expect educators to suffer in silence for the sake of reputation or convenience.

Why We Became Teachers

We didn't become teachers to endure abuse. We became teachers to inspire, to educate, to build futures. It's time to ensure that our schools are places where those dreams can thrive – not just for the students, but for the teachers who dedicate their lives to them.

If we don't demand change, if we don't stand up against violence, betrayal, and silence, then no one will. It's time to break the chains of complicity, speak out against the injustice, and refuse to settle for anything less than safety, dignity and respect. Our classrooms should be sanctuaries, not battlegrounds. And we deserve to teach without fear.

CHAPTER 17

THE HIDDEN BULLY

In the school environment, students are constantly reminded of the need to be respectful. The importance of kindness and empathy is highlighted in assemblies by the SLT, and in the classroom, teachers are expected to reinforce a zero-tolerance stance on bullying. Yet for many teachers, the reality behind the staffroom door is strikingly different. There is an unspoken truth in education – bullying isn't just an issue for students; it is rife amongst the staff body too. But while student bullying is addressed with clear policies and restorative conversations, bullying between colleagues is often met with silence, avoidance or – worse still – denial.

For some, this may come as a surprise. How can the same people who champion anti-bullying initiatives become the perpetrators of it? But the truth is that teaching is a pressure cooker of high expectations, endless scrutiny and performance-based judgment. It's a job where perfection is demanded but rarely achieved. In that crucible, cracks appear, and sometimes people behave in ways that betray their own values.

But this isn't about management bullying teachers. This is about the everyday interactions between classroom teachers – those of us in the trenches, navigating the same stress, the same students, the same long days. This is about the subtle yet damaging acts of colleague-on-colleague bullying.

The Quiet War in the Staffroom

Unlike the playground antics of children, adult bullying among teachers isn't the typical name-calling or physical shoving. It's quieter and more insidious. It's the heavy sigh when someone walks into a room, the exclusion from staffroom conversations, the collective eyeroll when a particular teacher offers an idea in a meeting. These actions, though subtle, chip away at confidence and create a culture of isolation.

According to a 2019 survey by the Teacher Wellbeing Index, over 25% of teachers reported being subjected to bullying or harassment in their workplace. The forms of bullying ranged from exclusion to gaslighting, with 21% of teachers stating that their bullying experience came directly from colleagues rather than management.

I once worked in a religious school where this was painfully obvious. There was a young, enthusiastic teacher – let's call her Katrina. She wasn't perfect, but she was passionate. She liked a particular style of music and dressed in a way that reflected that genre – nothing inappropriate for a school environment, but also not the standard office-wear that most teachers opted for. Despite this being her only real "crime", it didn't take long for the whispers to start.

These weren't direct confrontations – they were murmurs behind her back, shared glances exchanged in meetings and snide remarks made just loud enough for her to hear. One colleague said she was "allergic to her", a veiled joke that became a running line in the department office.

But here's the thing about workplace bullying – it's rarely straightforward. Bullies are skilled at shaping the narrative. When Katrina finally raised this with her line manager, after months of putting up with this treatment, her tormentors came armed with stories of "misunderstandings" and "miscommunication". They banded together, united in their version of events. And anyone who opposed them would be next in line.

If there's one word that has come to symbolise the gaslighting of bullied teachers, it's "misunderstanding". Somehow, the victim is always "confused" or "reading too much into it". It's never that the other teachers were being cruel – oh no – it's that the person on the receiving end just didn't get the joke or was too sensitive.

Katrina left the school after her reports to management went unheard. And while her departure went unnoticed by some, others used it as an example of "a teacher who just couldn't handle it." The irony, of course, is that Katrina handled the students just fine. It was the adults she couldn't survive.

Rumours and Reputations: The Currency of Control

There's a reason why gossip is sometimes referred to as "currency". In schools, information – and misinformation – can be traded like gold. Who's struggling with behaviour management, who's dating who, who might be on their way out. These conversations often have little to do with support or problem-solving; instead, they create a toxic staffroom pecking order, where the top dog is the one with the most gossip to trade and the veracity of those stories doesn't matter at all. If you are the subject of these rumours and staffroom conversations though, it can feel a hell of a lot like bullying. As one teacher lamented in a forum: "Backstabbing, toxicity, gossip...does anyone feel mentally violated at the end of a school day? I will take a job that pays half of my current salary if it cuts half of the misery. Desperate to get out." Statements like these are a testament to the emotional toll that an unhealthy school environment can take on educators, eroding their resilience and sense of worth.

According to research by the Education Support Partnership, over 60% of teachers reported experiencing gossip, exclusion or slander from colleagues at some point in their career. Unlike the visible bullying that students exhibit, this type of bullying hides in plain sight. It's disguised as "banter" or "just a joke".

Students can smell this tension. They see the power dynamics that adults try to hide. They know when a teacher is respected by their colleagues and when they aren't. And for some students, particularly those already skilled in manipulation, this becomes a weapon. If the staffroom has branded a teacher as "weak", students will double down on that narrative. After all, if even the adults don't respect Katrina, why should they?

Some students will even use social media to "dig up dirt" on teachers. They look for YouTube channels, social media handles, and anything they can weaponise. It's not uncommon for students to repeat gossip that started in the staffroom, reinforcing that teacher's perceived weakness.

How it Affects Mental Health

I've known teachers to break under the weight of this treatment. There's one teacher I'll never forget – let's call her Elizabeth. Elizabeth was brilliant. Passionate, organised and always prepared to go the extra mile for her students. She was loved by her students but disliked by a few of her colleagues for "trying too hard" and "acting like she's better than us". They saw her ambition as a threat, so they made it their mission to humble her.

Her initiatives were dismissed as "overcomplicating things" and requests for support were met with claims of "I'm too busy right now". If she stayed late, they rolled their eyes and said she was "just trying to be seen". If she left early, they'd mutter, "Must be nice to leave before 3:30."

Elizabeth withdrew. She stopped offering ideas in meetings, started asking for permission instead of using her initiative. Her confidence crumbled, and she took more sick days than usual. Her absence became the next source of gossip. "She's always off these days," they'd say, as if they hadn't played a role in driving her to this. By the time she resigned, they'd already rewritten her story. "She wasn't cut out for it."

According to Mind's 2022 Wellbeing in Education Report, 30% of teachers who experienced bullying from colleagues developed symptoms of anxiety or depression, with 16% considering leaving the profession entirely.

The Biggest Irony

Bullying and toxicity in workplace environments is not unique to teaching. Unlike some of the other issues explored in this book, this challenge is one faced by others in a number of professions. So why have I chosen to focus on it? Well, because of the irony of the fact that schools, and by extension, educators, preach the values of respect, empathy and kindness to the students in our care on a daily basis. Yet those values are not evident in the staffrooms of those very schools. The sheer hypocrisy of this situation is what makes the bullying culture amongst school staff so galling.

Teaching is a tough job. The pressure of constant deadlines, curriculum changes, parental scrutiny and challenging student behaviour can take its toll and cause some teachers to turn on each other. For some, it's about control. For others, it's survival. When you're all drowning, it's easier to push someone else under to keep yourself afloat.

And then there's insecurity. Some teachers fear change, fear new ideas, fear anyone who comes along with fresh perspectives. Bullying is their way of keeping things "as they are". New teachers with "big ideas" are targets because they challenge the status quo. Many newly qualified teachers report experiencing bullying or intimidation in their first two years of teaching (according to data from the NEU). The most cited reasons include being "too enthusiastic" or "not fitting in with the department culture."

The solution to this issue is not a simple one. It's not about just growing thicker skin. It's about creating the same safe environment for teachers that we demand for our students. Support systems, not silence. Intervention, not indifference. Schools must foster a culture where teachers can voice concerns without being labelled as "difficult" and staffroom pecking orders are a relic of the past. We must treat each other with the same respect, kindness and empathy that we promote in our classrooms and assemblies.

CHAPTER 18

AVOIDING WORK ROMANCE

Schools are uniquely intense environments. Long hours, high stress and shared challenges foster a sense of camaraderie that can easily blur the lines between professional and personal relationships. According to a Randstad Education survey, teachers are more likely than most professionals to engage in relationships with colleagues. But while these relationships may start in moments of shared struggle, they often end in situations that destabilise the entire school community.

Schools are microcosms of society, humming with whispered rumours, stolen glances, and alliances that could rival a political thriller. Forget reality TV or Netflix dramas – schools churn out scandals so fast, even Lady Whistledown would struggle to keep up. Headteachers and deputy heads, support staff and teachers, teachers and teachers – relationships abound, and some of them are the scandalous, illicit affairs you might imagine.

These relationships don't just raise eyebrows, they ripple through the entire institution, leaving chaos, divided staff, and disillusioned students in their wake. From sneaky coffee breaks to headline-worthy scandals, the story of staffroom relationships is less about happily-ever-after and more about the fallout that follows when personal lives collide with professional boundaries.

A Real-Life Example

Back in my sixth-form days, the headteacher, a married man with children, was rumoured to be having an affair with the deputy head – also married. Once this tidbit made its way into the student rumour mill, it exploded like wildfire. The corridors buzzed with whispers: from sneaky meetings in the staffroom to being "caught in the act" by the caretaker. While much of it was undoubtedly embellished, the fallout was real. The once-respected school leaders became tabloid fodder for teenagers, and the atmosphere descended into chaos. Staff were divided into factions, students lost respect, and the credibility of the school leadership was irreparably damaged.

For every workplace romance that ends happily-ever-after, countless others crash and burn, leaving collateral damage in their wake. When relationships implode, the toxicity spills into the staffroom, infecting professional collaborations and creating awkward interactions in front of students – who are, let's be honest, more observant than any adult gives them credit for. These aren't just personal issues – they're professional landmines that compromise the very fabric of the school. Because when a school becomes a battleground for messy relationships, the losers aren't just the teachers involved – it's everyone who has to endure the fallout.

I've heard stories that highlight just how messy these situations can become. One teacher left her husband for a colleague, only to find out he was secretly dating another staff member at the same school. Another staff member's affair with a senior leader was accidentally revealed when they were tagged in a photo on social media, leading to a public scandal that rocked the school. Then there was the department torn apart by a love triangle, with three colleagues dragging half the staff into their personal drama. These stories reveal the deeper issue of how private relationships, when mishandled, can destabilise an entire workplace.

Why Do Teachers Hook Up So Often?

It might sound like I'm exaggerating, but the statistics are real. According to a 2022 survey by Tes (the Times Educational Supplement), nearly 20% of teachers admitted to having a romantic relationship with a colleague at some point in their career. And how many more are still at it, sneaking glances over lesson plans and "accidentally" bumping into each other in the staffroom?

Then there's the factor of teacher burnout. Teaching is one of the most stressful jobs out there. In 2020, the Education Support Partnership reported that 84% of teachers described themselves as "stressed"[xiii] – more than surgeons and emergency responders. Stress has a way of making people seek relief, and for some, that means seeking solace in a forbidden workplace romance. Add in the adrenaline rush of sneaking around, and you've got a cocktail that's almost as addictive as a double shot of espresso during a Monday morning briefing.

Love in the Time of Timetables: A Recipe for Disaster

I once worked at a school where a relationship between two staff members spiralled into chaos, completely abandoning professionalism. What started as a harmless interaction quickly turned toxic, dragging the entire team into the destructive aftermath. The two went from colleagues to adversaries, and their personal issues spilled over into meetings, departmental decisions, and even lesson rotas. Restraining orders were filed, the police got involved, and staff had to rearrange schedules just to avoid them crossing paths. It didn't just disrupt their lives – it fractured the department, leaving a team distracted, divided and exhausted from navigating their dysfunction.

This wasn't a one-off occurrence – it's a brutal reality of blurred lines in a high-pressure environment. When staff members are involved in relationships, normal school boundaries are forgotten and the ripple effect can be disastrous. In one school I worked in, a "power couple" became inseparable, from break times to after-hours marking sessions. When they clashed, the tension was palpable. The atmosphere was suffocating, with everyone walking on eggshells trying not to set them off.

The Brutal Fallout of Staffroom Relationships

When relationships in schools go wrong (and they often do) the consequences are far more severe than the awkwardness of a typical workplace. In schools, you can't just avoid the person by taking a different route to the photocopier. You're trapped in a confined space with someone who used to be part of your personal life, and everyone around you is watching, whispering and waiting for the drama to unfold.

If you teach the same year group or share responsibilities, it's a logistical nightmare. The SLT are often forced to act like referees, reorganising meetings (if they are in the same department) and duty rotas to keep the peace. Every glance across the staffroom is scrutinised. Every interaction becomes fodder for student rumours, as Year 10s nudge each other in corridors and giggle about how two teachers are awkwardly avoiding each other.

Even worse are the scenarios involving senior leaders. When someone in a position of power gets romantically entangled with a subordinate, the fallout affects the entire staff. Accusations of favouritism and abuse of authority reverberate through the school, creating distrust and resentment among the team. In one case, a headteacher's affair with a TA became public knowledge, leading to whispered speculation that promotions were being handed out in exchange for personal loyalty rather than professional merit.

A Hard Lesson: Think Twice Before Mixing Work and Romance

If you're tempted to pursue a relationship with a colleague, ask yourself if you're ready to face the consequences. Can you endure the scrutiny of students, parents and colleagues? Can you handle the possibility of staffroom hostility, fractured alliances or even losing your job? In schools, nothing stays private for long, and your personal choices can quickly become everyone's business.

The stakes are higher in teaching. The gossip is relentless, and the consequences are far-reaching. If romance is on your mind, consider looking outside the school gates. Because in teaching, lessons aren't just for students – and sometimes, you're the one who learns the hardest truths.

CHAPTER 19

SUPPLY TEACHING – A THANKLESS ART

By now you've probably realised that teaching in the modern-day classroom can be a hazardous enterprise. But if you think the job of an ordinary classroom teacher is tough, then prepare yourself for an insight into an even more perilous occupation – that of the supply teacher.

Supply teaching introduces you to the unpolished underbelly of the education system, where every day feels like stepping into the Wild West. You're a gunslinger armed with only a whiteboard marker for a weapon, walking into unfamiliar territory to face off against the unpredictable, unruly and downright chaotic. There are no allies here, no safety nets, just a fragile hope that you'll survive the day relatively unscathed. Having navigated this minefield myself and swapped battle scars with fellow supply teachers, one truth is undeniable: this isn't a career for the faint-hearted or thin-skinned.

The Agency Hustle: Modern-Day Pirates

Supply teaching starts with signing up to an agency; those self-proclaimed "recruitment specialists" who are more like pirates in corporate attire. They lure you in with promises of flexibility and steady work, but the reality is that it's just a hustle designed to line their own pockets.

Agencies charge schools anywhere between £250 and £310 a day for your services, but you'll be lucky to see half of that. "The school's on a tight budget," they'll say, or "We're doing our best to get you more!" Meanwhile, they're laughing all the way to the bank, their biggest "costs" being Pret meal deals and those Instagram-worthy office perks.

And let's not forget the umbrella companies they use to keep you at arm's length. These setups ensure that they're not technically your employer, so good luck chasing fair treatment. The agency doesn't have to deal with the headaches of employment law or basic worker rights. They're the middlemen who cash in without any of the responsibility.

Oh, and if a school dares to like you enough to offer you a permanent role, don't think you're walking away scot-free. The agency will hit the school with a "finder's fee" ranging from £2,000 to £5,000 for the privilege of hiring you outright. It's like they're holding you hostage, and the ransom is ludicrous. And what do you, the teacher, get from that finder's fee? Not a single penny. The best they'll offer is a £150 referral fee if you rope another victim into their clutches – and even then, there's a list of conditions longer than the T&Cs of a streaming service that you have to meet in order to receive it.

Take Obi, a teacher who was offered £120 daily rate to work in a school with a "low-budget", according to his agent. Turns out, the agency was charging the school a whopping £310 daily. When Obi unexpectedly came into this knowledge (these transactions are notoriously cloak and dagger) and challenged the agency, they simply shrugged and mumbled something about "covering costs". Costs of what, their designer office chairs? Obi threatened to walk out, and suddenly, as if by magic, his daily rate jumped to £185.50. Funny how that works.

Tough Schools: The Real Hunger Games

Let's talk about the so-called "challenging schools" where supply teachers are often sent. These are environments where structure is fragile at best, chaos is the norm, and you're seen as a disposable stopgap. Walking into one of these schools, you quickly realise the students see you as an intruder, not a teacher. For some, you're an object of ridicule; for others, an opportunity for disruption.

In one school that I was drafted into in Thurrock, I was greeted with cheers the moment I walked in: "Yesss, supply teacher!" That wasn't enthusiasm, it was a warning that today would be a free-for-all. Before I'd even unpacked my bag, one student was hanging out of the window, another was blasting music on their phone and a third was interrogating me with, "Do you even know what you're doing?" The answer in that moment was no, I didn't. Because nothing prepares you for being thrown into the deep end with no support.

At another school in East London, I walked into a classroom only to find it transformed into a full-blown black-market emporium. Students were running an underground tuck shop with the finesse of Wall Street traders – Walkers crisps for £1.50 a bag, Skittles for £2, and, yes, vapes for a fiver. They even had a loyalty scheme, and one bold entrepreneur tried to bribe me with a "teacher's discount" if I turned a blind eye. Forget "challenging environments", this was a live-action episode of *Breaking Bad* set in a secondary school.

Supply Teachers: The Disposable Heroes

Respect is optional for supply teachers. You're not seen as a professional, you're the human duct tape slapped onto a broken system. Even when you show up, do your job and manage to maintain order, you're still the easiest scapegoat when things go wrong.

Take Alex, a supply teacher sent to a notoriously rough school in Dagenham for a two-week assignment. On day one he was threatened with violence and by day three, a student had pushed him into a door. Alex reported it, expecting support, but instead, the school dropped him without hesitation. His agency called that evening to say the school no longer needed his services. It's easier to fire the supply teacher than address the root problem.

Then there's Sarah, a supply teacher handed a timetable covering six subjects she wasn't qualified to teach, without resources or guidance. When she asked for support, the head of faculty shrugged and said, "Just keep them in the room and make sure no one dies". Inspirational leadership at its peak.

This brings me to my next, rather depressing, point. Supply teachers can often face as much discrimination and disrespect from the permanent staff in these schools, as from the students. Poor communication, dismissive attitudes and exclusion from staff areas are common complaints that supply teachers report, with some stating that it's the appalling treatment from so-called "colleagues" that would prevent them from returning to a school, rather than the behaviour of students. Maybe it's because, rightly or wrongly, we've come to expect disrespect from children and teenagers, but it's harder to forgive from adults in the same profession, who should know better.

The Perks...If You Can Call Them That

There are still some upsides to supply teaching. With day-to-day supply there's no marking, no parents' evenings and you can walk out at 3:30pm without needing to plan lessons for the next day. For some teachers, the lack of long-term commitment is also appealing. You're not tied to one school or embroiled in staff politics.

But let's not romanticise this; the financial instability and lack of professional recognition make it a deeply unfulfilling experience for many, and those so-called "perks" are offset by unrelenting disrespect and being treated as little more than a body in a chaotic classroom.

The often brutal and dehumanising treatment of supply teachers is reflected in the approach from their own agencies. Teaching agencies thrive on instability, exploiting the staffing crisis in schools to maximise their profits. They don't see you as a skilled professional or an individual with boundaries – they see you as a commodity to be sold to the highest bidder. Your qualifications, experience and mental health are secondary to their primary goal: keeping schools staffed at any cost to ensure their professional contracts remain intact.

Yes, you can leave at 3:30pm, but that freedom is hollow compensation for the chaos you're often thrown into. Toxic environments, unmanageable behaviour and non-existent support are common, and if you dare to speak up about the mental toll it's taking, don't expect sympathy. Agencies will brush off your concerns, prioritising their financial relationship with the school over your well-being. Worse still, they'll emotionally blackmail you, guilt-tripping you with lines like "the students need you" or "you're letting the school down," as if you owe loyalty to a system that has done nothing by treat you poorly. And don't think for a second that they'll fight for you. If the school no longer wants you, they'll drop you just as quickly. The message is clear – you're only as valuable as the profit you generate.

Grim Statistics

The data doesn't lie – supply teaching is often a short-lived career move. The National Education Union reports that one in five supply teachers quits within the first year. A Teacher Tapp survey revealed that 65% of supply teachers feel unsupported compared to their permanent counterparts. And let's be honest, those numbers probably underestimate the real frustration.

The Brutal Truth

Recently, the cover supervisor at my school confided to me that many supply teachers don't even last until break time. She said that things had gotten so bad that she is increasingly shocked if a supply teacher makes it to the final bell. If this isn't damning testimony, I don't know what is.

Supply teaching demands every ounce of strength and adaptability you can muster. You're dispensible in the education system, dropped into chaos with little support and even less respect. Agencies exploit you, schools barely tolerate you and students see you as either an easy target or a temporary inconvenience.

Yet, for all its flaws, supply teaching builds unparalleled resilience. It forces you to think on your feet, handle relentless pressure and adapt to whatever chaos greets you that day. It's a brutal crash course in survival, but if you can endure it, you'll thrive in any environment. Just don't expect gratitude, or even basic recognition, for navigating one of the toughest, most thankless roles in education.

Survival Tips for Supply Teachers

If you do find yourself in this perilous role, arm yourself with these top tips:

- **Pack Snacks and Patience** – long days and challenging behaviour will drain you. Keep your energy up and remember to breathe.

- **Document Everything** – keep a record of incidents. If something goes wrong, having the facts on paper is your only defence.

- **Beware the Cheer** – if the students cheer when you walk in, it's not a compliment. It's a warning.

- **Demand Fair Pay** – agencies will always try to lowball you. Know your worth and negotiate hard.

- **Plan an Exit Strategy** – always have a back-up plan. The system is as disposable to you as you are to it.

PART 5

SURVIVAL STRATEGIES – NAVIGATING THE PROFESSION

CHAPTER 20

HR – THE SMILING ASSASSIN

At my current school, HR is personified by a woman who could make a battle-hardened general flinch. She's not the type you laugh and joke with because, frankly, she doesn't do "banter". Her reputation precedes her: she takes no prisoners so you must follow the rules and bring receipts if you want to survive. And you know what? I respect that. You walk into her office armed with documents and rehearsed answers, bracing yourself like a defendant stepping into the dock, conscious that every word can dictate your fate. At least she's upfront about her role – to enforce policies and hold everyone accountable – no matter how intimidating that might be.

But other schools are a different beast entirely. HR may come wrapped in niceness; offering you tea and a biscuit, chatting about the weather and pretending they're your mate. They'll smile sweetly while reviewing your entire employment history, probably highlighting every email you sent with a typo. They're like a stealth bomber: no warning, no sound – just a polite nod and then boom, you're summoned to a meeting that starts with, "This is just an informal chat". Spoiler alert: it's never "just an informal chat".

HR Isn't There for You

Let me be clear: HR is not your friend. Their job is to protect the school's interests, and when I say "school's interests," what I really mean is the interests of senior management – whether that's managing staff or, in some cases, manipulating them. Think of HR as the executioner in a medieval court: technically impartial, but you know whose orders they're following. Sure, they might look sympathetic when you unload your frustrations about a toxic department or an unhinged line manager, but don't mistake that for loyalty. Every word you say is catalogued, timestamped and ready to be weaponised the moment it suits them.

Take this one account I heard. A teacher, let's call her Ms Bailey, confided in HR about feeling overwhelmed by her workload and unsupported by her department. The HR representative nodded, tilted their head at just the right angle of "empathetic understanding", and even slid over a box of tissues for good measure. They reassured her, "We're here to help," in that syrupy tone that makes you want to believe them. Fast forward two weeks and Ms Bailey is yanked into a performance review meeting where her heartfelt concerns were magically transformed into "evidence" of her "inability to cope with professional responsibilities". That's HR in action: not helpers, but spin doctors armed with a briefcase full of euphemisms.

If an HR representative ever smiles at you and says, "We're here to support you," assume you're one step away from being shown the door. At my current school, at least you know you're going into battle. HR doesn't sugarcoat. If you're in trouble, they tell you outright, giving you a fighting chance to prepare. But at other schools, that smile is a Trojan horse, hiding a meticulously crafted plan to offload you without so much as a ripple in their Ofsted report.

One teacher I know – let's call him Mike – was told HR wanted to "discuss his future career development". He walked into the meeting optimistic, thinking they might offer him a new role or some CPD. Instead, he walked out with a "mutual agreement" to leave, signed and sealed before he even knew what was happening. They played him like a fiddle and even wished him luck in his "future endeavours" with a straight face.

The Hidden Agenda

And let's not forget the thinly veiled agenda. If a headteacher wants you "managed out", HR will happily play the enforcer, ensuring the process is wrapped in just enough procedural fluff to avoid any legal backlash. They'll nod along, jot down notes, and then produce a perfectly worded report designed to make your exit look like it was your idea all along. It's not about what's best for the school as a whole, and it's certainly not about what's best for you. It's about protecting the people in power while making it look like everything's above board.

So, before you step into an HR meeting thinking you're walking into a space of neutral arbitration, remember this: HR isn't there to fix your problems. They're there to ensure the school survives – preferably with as little damage to its reputation (and senior management) as possible. And if you're not careful, you'll find yourself the scapegoat for issues you didn't even know existed.

HR and Policies: A Loaded Weapon

Most teachers don't read policies until they're in trouble, which is like waiting until your house is on fire to read the manual for a fire extinguisher. HR loves policies because they're the ultimate weapon in their arsenal. If you're on their radar for the wrong reasons and you so much as sneeze in a way that violates a code of conduct, they'll pounce. And if they can't find a direct violation, they'll hit you with something vague, like "bringing the school into disrepute".

Case in point: an outspoken teacher I worked with was once reprimanded for "improper use of technology". He had forgotten to lock his laptop, and a student emailed a love letter to another student from his email account. HR swooped in like they'd cracked a major international cybercrime ring. Despite this being a relatively minor human error, he was given a written warning which was placed on his file for 12 months, a disciplinary action that ultimately led to him missing out on a job opportunity in another school and subsequently leaving the profession altogether. Policies aren't there to protect you; they're there to ensure the school has something to point to when things go south.

Survival Tips for Dealing with HR

- **Know the Policies** – Read every policy, twice. Know them better than HR does, because ignorance isn't just bliss – it's career suicide.

- **Document Everything** – Every email, every conversation, every incident. Keep it all. If HR comes knocking, you'll need receipts.

- **Stay Professional** – Even if you're seething inside, stay calm. HR thrives on emotional outbursts to paint you as "unprofessional".

- **Bring a Union Rep** – Always, always bring someone with you to any HR meeting. Think of them as your legal counsel in a courtroom.

- **Trust Your Gut** – If something feels off, it probably is. HR is rarely involved unless there's a problem, and that problem could very well be you.

The Bottom Line

HR isn't there to ensure the school thrives, they're there to make sure management can "deal with" teachers without the school ending up on the wrong side of a tribunal. It's less about supporting you and more about safeguarding the institution's reputation and minimising liability. Schools might still survive without HR, but they'd probably see fewer neatly orchestrated exits and more SLT scrambling to cover their own backs.

At its core, HR exists to enable management to tick boxes, avoid legal challenges and enforce policies that are often wielded as weapons rather than tools of support. They're not the safety net you hope for, so if you're walking into an HR meeting, remember: their job isn't to protect you, but to ensure the school survives the fallout. Always come prepared – and definitely skip the biscuit.

CHAPTER 21

THE EDUCATOR'S SURVIVAL TOOLKIT

If you're a teacher that has made it this far and are still thinking, "This isn't something I've experienced. This isn't something I've witnessed" then, as I've said before, you're one of the lucky ones. But if you have felt the crushing weight of juggling impossible deadlines, managing unpredictable students, trying to appease demanding parents and enduring management's relentless obsession with data, I hope this book has made you realise that you're not alone.

You're part of a vast and growing army of educators battling to keep their heads above water in a system that too often feels rigged against us. Don't believe me? Just look at the 174,000 members (and counting) of the Facebook group *Life After Teaching – Exit the Classroom and Thrive*. That number isn't just a statistic – it's a sign of how many of us are questioning how much more we can take.

This chapter is about what I've learned – the strategies I've observed, used and refined to survive every institution I've worked in. This is your battle plan: no fluff, no platitudes, just practical advice born from experience. It's your toolkit to not only stay afloat, but hopefully, to keep moving forward and even thrive.

1. Do Your Homework Before Signing Anything

Do your homework – or pay the price. Accepting a teaching position without digging deep into the school's ethos, staff turnover and working culture is a dangerous leap into the unknown. Speak to current staff, scrutinise Ofsted reports, and look beyond the polished façade of prospectuses and recruitment adverts. High turnover and perennial vacancies aren't coincidental, they scream of poor leadership, burnout and a culture that grinds teachers down. In a profession where nearly 40% leave within five years, joining the wrong school isn't just a misstep – it can be disastrous. Don't let league tables and shiny slogans blind you to the red flags. Your professional future and well-being deserve better.

A school that doesn't value its staff as much as its students will destroy you. No amount of resilience can protect you from an environment driven by fear, micromanagement and relentless pressure to meet unrealistic expectations. Do the work now before you're locked into a toxic contract, and ensure you're stepping into a role that fosters growth and respect – not exhaustion and regret.

2. Read the School Policies – Knowledge is Power (and Self-Protection)

School policies are not your safety net; they're the fine print which can be weaponised against you. Rarely are they clearly communicated, yet they're the first thing wielded against you when cracks appear. Ignorance is not bliss – it's potentially professional suicide. From safeguarding to behaviour management, every line you fail to read is a prospective pitfall, waiting to be exploited when senior leadership needs a scapegoat. Policies aren't static – they're malleable tools for deflecting blame, often at the expense of teachers left unsupported on the front line.

Take ownership of your survival – know every clause, every expectation and every loophole. When the storm hits, and it will, your best defence isn't hope, it's preparation. Forewarned is forearmed, so while the policies themselves won't protect you, knowing them inside out just might.

3. HR Isn't Your Friend – Approach with Caution

Remember, HR isn't there to protect you. Their priority is to safeguard the institution's interests. Any interaction, no matter how informal it seems, should be approached with caution. "Check-ins" or casual conversations are rarely about your well-being; they're often about gathering information. If HR suddenly starts taking an interest in you, it's usually the prelude to a performance review, disciplinary action or an attempt to quietly manage you out. Keep your interactions professional and document everything – no matter how insignificant it may seem at the time. Don't let the appearance of transparency be your downfall.

4. Don't Rush for a Promotion

Climbing the ladder in teaching may seem like a cause for celebration, but the reality is often far from joyous: more responsibility means endless emails, mounting pressure and a constant stream of people demanding answers to problems you didn't create. Studies show that 80% of UK teachers experience severe stress, with middle-management roles often being a one-way ticket to burnout. These positions frequently come with extra duties disguised as "opportunities", but rarely provide adequate support or fair renumeration. Before accepting a promotion, consider the toll it will take on your time, health and well-being – progression can be a positive move, but go into it with your eyes open.

5. Document Like Your Life Depends on It

Teaching is unpredictable – one moment you're delivering a lesson, the next you're defending yourself in a meeting about "failing to connect with a student". In this profession, where everything you say or do can be dissected, misinterpreted or held against you, documentation shouldn't be viewed as a chore – it's your armour. A parent explodes in frustration? Record it. A vague "friendly reminder" from the SLT about your conduct? Save it. You're not being paranoid, you're being astute, preparing for a day that you hope won't come, but you're ready for if it does. One well-timed email, one detailed log, one saved memo can mean the difference between safeguarding your reputation and facing irreversible consequences. For your professional self-preservation, meticulous record-keeping is essential.

6. Avoid Being Alone with a Student (If You Can)

Safeguarding policies should be in place to protect members of staff as much as the students in their care. While it is unfortunate that teachers may have to think twice before offering extra support to students if it means that they'll be alone in a classroom with them, this is something you must consider to avoid placing yourself in a vulnerable position, or leaving yourself open to a potentially malicious accusation. If you cannot avoid these situations, keep doors open, remain in public or monitored spaces and ensure transparency at all times. Even the most trivial interaction, twisted by perception or malice, could shatter your reputation and mental health beyond repair. Don't take the risk.

7. Skip the Gossip

The staffroom may seem like a safe space, but it's often a breeding ground for whispers and power-plays. Gossip flows freely, and while it may appear harmless it can quickly spiral, with damaging consequences. One off-hand comment can be repeated out of context or weaponised against you. Conversations about senior leadership or other staff members often travel up the chain, leaving you exposed. The hard truth is not everyone sitting beside you is on your side. Stay professional, observe and keep personal opinions to yourself – what feels like camaraderie today could become ammunition tomorrow.

8. Avoid Social Media Like the Plague

One poorly judged post or photo on social media can end your teaching career in an instant. Adding students as friends is a clear violation of boundaries, and even connecting with colleagues online can blur the lines between personal and professional lives. A single tagged photo from a staff social event could spiral into unwanted scrutiny, putting your professionalism in jeopardy. The stark reality is that many teachers have faced disciplinary action, lost their jobs or irreparably damaged their reputations through social media missteps. Keep your personal life strictly private, because in teaching, even the smallest lapse in judgment can have devastating consequences.

9. Bring Receipts to Parents' Evening

Parents' evening often feels less like a constructive dialogue and more like standing in the dock, where parents play the role of prosecutors, armed with expectations and accusations. Every missed target, every underwhelming grade and every behavioural incident becomes evidence in a case against your professionalism, regardless of the hours spent adapting lessons, offering interventions or chasing engagement from a student who barely lifts a pen. Without meticulous documentation – grades, incident logs and attendance records – you risk becoming the scapegoat for issues that stem from a lack of accountability beyond the classroom.

It's a draining exercise, one that exposes a brutal truth: for some parents, the focus isn't the student's growth but shifting the weight of responsibility. To avoid being a convenient fall-guy, make sure you have your paperwork in order and the data to support your constructive comments.

10. Build Alliances with Parents

Engaging with parents isn't about ticking a box; it's the difference between fostering a supportive partnership and enduring endless resistance. Be brutally transparent – share the details of their child's progress, both the positive developments and any setbacks, without sugar-coating or evading difficult conversations. Parents are naturally defensive, but if they see you're invested in their child's success, they're more likely to meet you halfway. When tensions flare, don't waste time on blame games. Focus on actionable solutions that put the student at the heart of the conversation. With the right approach, a combative parent can become an ally, collaborating with you to strengthen your efforts rather than undermine them.

11. Embrace AI, Don't Fear It

AI isn't the villain of the classroom – it's an untapped resource we've been too cautious to trust. If misused, it can erode authenticity, but wielded wisely, it can transform the way we teach and lead. From streamlining lesson planning to creating truly personalised interventions, AI has the potential to lighten the relentless workload that many of us are struggling to bear.

It's also important to embrace this technology in order to prepare students for a world that demands its use. Ignoring AI isn't an option. Our students are increasingly using it, so if we don't teach them to harness it as a tool rather than a shortcut, we leave them vulnerable to dependency and misuse. Integrate it into your practice, model its ethical use, and show them that AI doesn't diminish their efforts; it can amplify them.

Far from being a threat to teaching, the use of AI can be viewed as a means to redefine it. The question isn't whether AI will change education, but whether we'll have the courage to shape how it does that.

12. Join a Union

If you're a teacher and you're not a member of a union, you're leaving yourself defenceless in a profession where defences are sadly required. Unions aren't perfect, far from it, but they are often the only shield between you and a system that prioritises institutional optics over individual wellbeing. Schools have entire legal teams on a retainer, ready to protect their interests at all costs. Who's protecting yours?

The harsh truth is that the education system is a labyrinth of policies and protocols, and without union support, you're navigating it blindfolded. Even unions can't always prevent injustice, but they are your first and often only line of defence against unfair treatment, safeguarding your rights when everything else is designed to erode them. If you're not in one, you're gambling with your career – and the odds aren't in your favour.

13. Don't Go to Work Unless You're Fit Enough

Do not step into a classroom unless you're fighting fit. Teaching is unforgiving, and limping through the day on fumes only guarantees one thing: mistakes that could have been avoided. You'll jeopardise your own health, lower your professional standards, and risk creating an unhealthy culture where exhaustion is seen as commitment. Schools will survive without you for a day or two – burnout is far more damaging, both to you and the students relying on your clarity and presence.

Taking time to recover is not a sign of weakness, but a responsible course of action. Prioritising your health ensures you come back stronger, sharper and capable of doing the job well. Dragging yourself in at less than your best is martyrdom, not professionalism. There's nothing heroic about a frazzled teacher. Know your limits, respect them and model the importance of self-care for the very students you're teaching to thrive.

14. Fight for Work-Life Balance and Protect your Mental Health

As we have established, teaching will demand everything you have and more, if you let it. The relentless pace, endless marking and unceasing pressures can strip you of your identity, leaving you a shell of who you once were. Burnout doesn't knock politely; it crashes in, bringing exhaustion and resentment along for the ride. If you don't fight for a work-life balance, no one else will do so on your behalf. You cannot pour from an empty cup, and pretending to be invincible only exacerbates the problem.

Reclaim your evenings and weekends. Shut down your email after hours, protect your lunch break like it's sacred, and carve out space for the things that make you feel human again. Draw your lines and hold them firm. Work will still be there tomorrow; your sanity might not. Lean on your loved ones, reach out to a counsellor or confide in a trusted colleague when the cracks begin to show. Prioritise yourself, because if you're not at your best, your students suffer too.

15. Know Your Gatekeepers

The backbone of every school are the support staff and admin team who hold the keys to its smooth operation. They are more than cogs in the machine – they are your frontline allies, often privy to the undercurrents of the institution long before they become noticeable. Their insights can illuminate the hidden fault lines of school politics, offer early warnings about looming issues and guide you through the minefield of tricky student cases or bureaucratic hurdles. Neglect them at your peril. These are the individuals who can open doors or keep them firmly shut, so it's in your best interests to befriend them – you won't regret it.

16. Celebrate Small Wins

In the chaotic world of teaching, where exhaustion and endless demands often drown out the good, it's easy to forget what truly matters. But every quiet breakthrough – a hesitant hand raised, a struggling learner finally finding the answer, a heartfelt "thank you" from a parent – offers moments that can sustain us. They're not just "small wins"; they're lifelines. Fail to recognise or celebrate them, and you risk losing sight of why you chose this profession in the first place.

Document these glimmers of progress, however trivial they might seem. Keep the thank you cards and revisit them when the grind feels unbearable. Because let's be brutally honest: without these reminders of impact, teaching can become a hollow, soul-destroying routine. These moments are your armour against disillusionment; the proof that the battle is worth fighting. Don't dismiss them – celebrate them.

17. Develop Resilience to External Expectations

It's with the best will in the world that I say: you are not a magician. Teaching is not a stage where you can conjure miracles to fix every failing system, every broken home or every disengaged child. Outcomes are shaped by a tangled web of external influences beyond your control, yet you are often expected to carry the weight of the world on your shoulders. Stop. Your duty is to give your best within the boundaries of what's achievable, not to self-destruct chasing impossible expectations.

When criticism or relentless scrutiny gnaws at your resolve, anchor yourself in the reason you stepped into this profession. Reconnect with the fire that first lit your passion for teaching – the drive to shape lives, not save systems. Let that clarity cut through the deafening noise of others' demands. Learn to say no.

18. Know When to Walk Away

If a school no longer values you, recognise the reality and leave. The system is not built for fairness but engineered for self-preservation, and fighting it will drain you – mentally, emotionally and professionally. Know when to step back. Your mental health and self-esteem are not worth sacrificing over a job – you will find another. Walk away before you're robbed of your passion, purpose and peace of mind. Choose yourself over a system that won't.

PART 6

A REFLECTION ON TEACHING – CHALLENGES AND HOPE

CHAPTER 22

TEACHING WITHOUT BORDERS

For many educators, the prospect of teaching abroad offers a beacon of hope – a chance to escape the unrelenting pressures of Ofsted inspections, the weight of unattainable targets and the relentless cycle of marking, meetings and data-driven expectations that dominate teaching in England. It feels like an opportunity to rediscover the essence of teaching: creativity, passion and a genuine connection with students, free from the often stifling grind of the UK education system.

However, stepping into a classroom in another country comes with its own set of complexities. Teaching abroad is a delicate balance of wonder, adaptation and, at times, frustration. Cultural differences can challenge even the most seasoned educator, while navigating unfamiliar bureaucracies and adjusting to the expectations of students and parents (whose perspectives on education may be completely different) can be both humbling and overwhelming.

Yet, for those who embrace the uncertainties, teaching abroad can become a journey of personal and professional growth. It offers a fresh perspective on education and often rekindles the joy of teaching, even if the challenges sometimes feel just as significant as those left behind.

These are the stories of teachers who stepped beyond their comfort zones, trading familiarity for the unknown. For every account of struggle, there is one of triumph; for every moment of doubt, a breakthrough. Together, they paint a picture of what it means to be a teacher in a global context, navigating new systems, surviving the challenges and redefining their roles as teachers in classrooms far from home.

Dubai

"Moving to Dubai to teach has been transformative for me and my family. For the first time in years, I've said goodbye to the Sunday night dread – even the night before my first day or when the students returned, I felt calm. Work is hard, and the days are long, but there's a positivity here that's hard to explain.

I can actually teach! My students genuinely want to learn, regardless of their ability or background. I only need to give instructions once – there's no constant stopping to address behaviour. Even my own children now describe school as "fun".

Technology is a big focus here. We use AI to create songs, boost engagement and even trial marking! Every student brings their own device, but traditional written work is still prioritised.

The work-life balance is still something I'm working on. The days are long – we leave for school at 6:30a.m. and return by 4:30p.m. – but the half-day Fridays and longer Christmas, summer and Eid breaks help. My husband isn't working at the moment and he's been our anchor, providing emotional and practical support while I focus on work.

What really stands out though, is how much happier people seem here. Maybe it's the weather, or maybe it's the lifestyle, but everyone I've met so far – at work and in public – has been friendly and willing to help.

If you're considering teaching abroad, I'd highly encourage you to take the leap. Dubai has its challenges, but the rewards are incredible."

- Paige, international teacher in Dubai

Australia

"I took the plunge and left the UK to teach in Australia, and the work-life balance is on another level. I start at 8:15, finish by 3:15, and I'm on the beach by 3:45 🏖️. Back in the UK, I was UP3 with endless responsibilities, but now I'm earning double, and my only task is to teach 🐯. Here, they truly value and trust their teachers. They want the best for the kids, but the pressure is nothing like what I experienced before. If you're considering the move, I can't recommend it enough!"

- Sarah, UK teacher turned Aussie educator

USA

"As someone who's taught in both the US and the UK, I've noticed the challenges are different but equally significant. In the US, the workload can feel more manageable; it's common to teach multiple sections of the same grade, which isn't as frequent in the UK. Teaching there also tends to be more student-centered and interactive – though that might just reflect my personal experience.

However, safeguarding in the US is a major concern. It's not taken as seriously as it is here in the UK, and there's often little capacity to properly follow up on reported concerns about students. Work-life balance is another issue. Taking sick days or time off is heavily frowned upon. I remember having a formal meeting after using just five of my ten sick days by March, where it was suggested I stop taking them so it wouldn't jeopardise my job or tenure.

And then, there's the reality of weapons. Guns are a very real concern. I grew up attending US public schools, where we had multiple real lockdowns because of gunshots in the neighbourhood. As a teacher, I had to lead lockdown drills – and also lived through actual lockdowns. The stress of that is incomparable. When I think about the school shootings I know of and the risks that come with teaching in the US, it makes me question if I could ever return to teaching there. The UK has its stresses, but I feel safer here in ways that truly matter."

– Emily, US teacher now working in the UK

China

"I taught in China, specifically in Shanghai, at a prestigious international school. Professionally, it was a fantastic experience. The resources were top-notch, the students were eager to learn, and the support from leadership was exceptional. The pay was excellent, and the opportunity to work with colleagues from around the world enriched my teaching practice in ways I hadn't anticipated.

However, the overall quality of life outside of school was challenging. Shanghai is a vibrant city, but the constant crowds, relentless traffic and the ever-present haze of pollution made it difficult to truly relax. Green spaces were hard to come by, and the lack of nature meant I rarely had the chance to disconnect from the urban hustle. Life felt fast-paced and overwhelming, with little room for serenity or reflection.

While the school itself was a haven of academic excellence, it was hard to ignore the stress of daily life in such a densely populated metropolis. Over time, this took a toll on me and many of my expat colleagues. Despite the professional rewards, the personal challenges led us to move on, seeking a better balance between work and life."

— Marcus, English teacher in Shanghai

Scotland

"Teaching in Scotland often gets romanticised as being better than in England, but the truth is, the challenges are just as relentless, if not worse. Sure, we have differences, like directed hours and working time agreements, but day-to-day school life is marked by the same struggles.

Budget cuts are biting harder every year, leaving us with fewer support staff and resources. Most teachers I know are dipping into their own pockets to buy essential materials, which is heartbreaking. And let's not even start on the paperwork – it's endless. There's an obsession with data over actual children, and the lack of support for pupils in crisis is gut-wrenching. We're seeing behavioural issues spiral, and teachers are expected to somehow manage without proper backing.

Then there's the management culture. I've worked in schools where passive-aggressive, micromanaging senior leaders treat staff as expendable. It's not just my experience either – friends across Scotland, in different schools and even local authorities, share the same stories.

Our working time agreements are supposed to set clear boundaries, outlining tasks and hours, but in reality, they're a joke. You'll see a job listed as "two hours" on paper, but it takes ten in practice. And yet, despite the official 35-hour week, most of us are working far beyond that, unpaid and unacknowledged.

Staffing is another nightmare. In rural areas, schools are scraping by, with supply teachers almost non-existent. If someone's off, classes get split, probationers are pulled in on their development days, or Support for Learning teachers are yanked from their interventions to cover – leaving their carefully planned pupil support in the bin. Meanwhile, in the central belt, there's the opposite problem: too many teachers fighting for limited jobs, with some schools cutting corners just to save money instead of bringing in supply.

All of this happens while we're being told to "improve attainment" and given lip service about staff wellbeing. It feels like a façade. The system says it values us, but the reality shows something very different. Teaching here can be fulfilling, but it's exhausting and demoralising when you're constantly stretched to breaking point."

– Greg, English teacher working in the Highlands

Jamaica

"Teaching in Jamaica is a serious undertaking, grounded in a culture where respect is deeply embedded. Students understand boundaries and discipline is rarely questioned. The workload, however, is relentless. Exams shape the entire educational journey, demanding a constant state of readiness from both students and teachers. It's like living in a world where GCSE-level pressure (in their case CXC) exists every year of a child's life. But beyond the grades, teaching here is about connection. It's about mentorship, guidance and being a steady presence for students who look to you for more than just lessons. Resources may be limited, but heart and determination fill the gaps."

- Donovan, Jamaican teacher

Thailand

"Teaching in Thailand has been a revelation! Living in Bangkok is full of surprises, and despite taking a pay cut on paper, the low tax rate (I'm paying just 11%) means I actually take home more than I did in the UK on UPS. But it's the work-life balance that's the real game changer. Evenings and weekends are mine again – no endless marking or planning. This Christmas, I'll be relaxing on an idyllic beach. Bliss!

What I love most is the low-stress approach to teaching here. It's built into the school's vision, and it shows. The kids are still learning loads, but the focus is on making teaching and learning enjoyable. For the first time in years, I'm having fun in the classroom, and so are my students."

- Elliot, international teacher in Thailand

"There are some excellent EYFS settings and a fantastic lifestyle to be had, but not all schools are great. My advice is to do your homework before making the move. You don't want to jump from one fire to another. That said, after this experience, there's no way I could ever return to teaching in the UK!"

- Julie, international teacher in Thailand

Teaching abroad isn't always the magical escape many envision, but it undeniably offers opportunities for transformation. The challenges are significant, and the pressures sometimes resemble those left behind, albeit in a different context. Yet for many educators who make the leap, the rewards can outweigh the difficulties. Recent data indicates that nearly 30% of UK teachers who move abroad cite improved financial circumstances as a key motivator, with destinations such as the UAE and China offering remuneration packages up to 40% higher than the UK average, alongside benefits like tax-free salaries and subsidised housing.

However, teaching overseas is about more than just financial gain. For some, it's a short-term opportunity to recharge and reflect; for others, it becomes a long-term career shift. Whether embracing innovative teaching strategies, navigating diverse classrooms or rediscovering the joy of teaching, working abroad provides a unique lens through which to view education. It can be a transformative experience that reshapes perspectives and renews purpose.

CHAPTER 23

THE GREAT ESCAPE

This chapter might feel like a detour, but after years of teaching – after you've taught, survived and repeated until your sanity's dangling by a thread – you start to wonder: *Is there more to life than this?* More than marking essays, playing referee in what feels like Netflix's latest crime drama, or calculating which tree on your commute would cause just enough damage to grant you a "mental health break" without actually ending it all? Yes, I'm talking about *the* tree. You know the one. Every teacher has one – the one you drive past daily, thinking, "Just a nudge... not too hard, but just enough for a week off". It's not funny, but somehow it is. Teaching: the only job where vehicular sabotage constitutes self-care.

Eventually you realise, *I can't do this anymore.* The burnout. The bureaucracy. The endless staff meetings that could've been emails. The performance reviews. And then, one day, you wake up and think, *surely there's life beyond this chaotic, caffeine-fuelled carousel of despair?*

And then you discover the group *Life After Teaching – Exit the Classroom and Thrive* on Facebook, like I did. It's like a digital group hug for teachers on the brink – or those who've already leapt off the cliff into the unknown. I like to call it the social media equivalent to *I'm a Teacher, Get Me Out of Here!* The posts in that group are a rollercoaster of hope, heartbreak and unfiltered honesty. Some make you laugh, others make you cry, and a few will have you clutching your chest while you hyperventilate.

One post stopped me dead in my tracks:

"Hi all. Feeling a bit stuck. I used to love my job, and I do love my colleagues and (most of) the kids. But it is tough. I had a mental breakdown a year ago, due to health, work and relationships. I spent months feeling suicidal and was off work for five months. I'm back teaching full-time and much better. I just don't know what I'd do other than teaching. I left finance to go into teaching and wouldn't go back because it's so unfulfilling. At 44, I just can't see myself teaching for another 20 years. Anyone who has made the jump, I'd be interested to hear what jobs you've gone for. PS – no kids myself, or partner, so I'm pretty flexible".

This post is brutally honest, and it captures a reality many teachers face: the soul-crushing question of "What now?" You pour your soul into teaching, only to wake up one day and realise it's drained you dry. The passion has gone, the burnout has set in and the idea of doing it for another 20 years gives you anxiety, BUT you have no idea what to do instead.

The Mid-Career Crisis

Teaching has a knack for drawing you in with promises of meaning and purpose. Damn those advertisements from Get Into Teaching: *Change lives! Inspire the next generation!* But after years of jumping through endless hoops, drowning in marking and wrestling with SLT demands, the rose-tinted glasses come crashing down, leaving you with nothing but exhaustion and a mildly concerning eye twitch.

The problem is teaching is all-consuming; it becomes your identity. When you leave, you're not just changing careers – you're untangling yourself from something that's been a part of you for years. And when you're in your 40s or 50s, it can feel incredibly daunting to not only have to start again professionally, but also reinvent yourself personally in the process.

Posts like the one above highlight the sheer terror of leaving teaching. It's not just about finding a new job; it's about finding yourself. The fear is real:

- "What skills do I even have outside of teaching?"
- "What if I end up in a soul-sucking corporate job?"
- "Am I too old to start over?"
- "Who am I if I'm not a teacher?"

Let me tell you, regardless of the subject area or age group that you specialise in, the panic is universal.

What Happens When You Leave?

Leaving teaching is like escaping a cult. At first, you're euphoric. *No marking! No behaviour policies! No Sunday-night dread!* But then reality sets in. You're on LinkedIn, desperately trying to make "can manage 30 teenagers without crying" sound like a marketable skill. The rejection emails roll in, and you start googling "Is dog walking a viable career?"

A key theme in online teaching forums like the aforementioned Facebook group, is the mixed bag of post-teaching experiences:

The Survivors

These are the ones who escaped teaching but aren't exactly skipping through fields of daisies. Think admin roles, HR positions or charity work. They've traded chaos for monotony, and while the daily grind no longer involves confiscating vape pens or arguing over uniform violations, it's not all sunshine and rainbows.

Take Melanie, who now works in HR for a local company. She's grateful she no longer wakes up with a knot in her stomach on Monday mornings, but her new reality includes endless meetings where "team synergy" is discussed as though it's the cure for world hunger. And the scariest part is the feeling that she's swapped one hamster wheel for another. Melanie spends her days wrestling with spreadsheets, wondering if she's doomed to die of boredom instead of burnout.

The Thrivers

These are the rare few who not only escaped teaching but found a new passion that pays the bills and doesn't slowly eat away at their souls.

Meet Dave, who left primary school teaching in February 2024 after ten years in the classroom. He's now a full-time videographer and photographer, living a life most of us can only dream about. His Instagram is a mix of perfectly captured sunsets, stunning wedding shots, and him sipping espresso in quaint cafés. The caption on his recent post reads: "From lesson plans to lens flares – best decision of my life".

Dave's joy is palpable, and enviable. While former colleagues are still stuck in staff meetings discussing literacy targets,

Dave's biggest concern is whether to shoot in natural light or bring out his studio setup. He's proof that sometimes, leaving teaching isn't just survival – it's a metamorphosis of epic proportions.

Then there's Emma, a former secondary school English teacher who walked out of her classroom in December 2023 and straight into a role in instructional design for an ed-tech company. Within months, she was creating interactive online courses, sitting at her laptop in her kitchen, wearing pyjamas to work and living her best life.

Her LinkedIn posts are always cheerful: "From marking essays to shaping the future of online learning! #Blessed #WorkFromHomeLife".

Emma's schedule now revolves around her morning coffee ritual, flexible deadlines, walking her dog on her lunch break and occasionally, a cheeky mid-afternoon yoga session.

She's earning more than she did as a teacher, working fewer hours, and now has more time for herself, her partner and her children. The only students she deals with are virtual avatars, and none of them have ever told her that her lesson was "bare boring".

Emma's story is the ultimate eat-your-heart-out moment for her former colleagues. Like Dave, she is proof that leaving teaching isn't just about survival – it can be a one-way ticket to a much happier existence.

The Broken

Now for the cautionary tales. These are the stories of people who left teaching, full of hope, only to find themselves in a waking nightmare.

Take James, who quit his secondary school teaching role in August 2023, fed up with endless marking and SLT micromanagement. With no plan and a lot of optimism, he landed a job in a call centre, thinking: *at least I won't have to deal with kids anymore.* Little did he know, it would be far worse.

James now spends his days apologising to irate strangers for problems he didn't cause – missed deliveries, broken appliances and one memorable call where someone threatened to sue him personally because of damage to their kitchen worktop caused by a faulty appliance. Every evening, James collapses onto his sofa, consumed by the terrifying realisation that he's stuck. He dreams of going back to teaching but fears it's too late.

And then there's Claire, who left her teaching job in search of "something easier" and ended up as a manager in a high-street shop. She thought swapping essays for folding jeans would be a breeze. She was wrong. A fight broke out in her store over a pair of discounted trainers, and she had to physically separate two customers – one of whom bit her. Now, every time Claire walks past a school, she feels an overwhelming pang of regret.

The Broken don't just wish they'd stayed, they haunt Facebook groups with warnings like, *"Don't leave unless you know exactly where you're going – because it's bleak out here".*

Why Leaving Feels So Hard

As previously established, teaching is more than a job: it's your identity. You're accustomed to being "the teacher" wherever you go, whether it's the supermarket or a family gathering. Leaving the profession can therefore feel like you are losing a huge part of yourself and can cause some to question who they actually are without that job title.

Many teachers leave teaching feeling utterly lost. The system has conditioned us to believe that our skills only belong in a classroom, which is utter nonsense. Teachers are some of the most skilled, adaptable and resourceful professionals out there. But finding a way to sell those highly transferable skills to the outside world is the real hurdle that many struggle to overcome.

If you're thinking of leaving teaching, know this: you're not alone. Thousands of teachers have walked this path before you. Some thrived, some survived and some regretted their choices. But what unites all of them is resilience. Teaching might be one of the toughest industries to work in, but it also builds a strength you didn't know you had.

CHAPTER 24
THE UNSUNG HEROES OF EDUCATION

By now you probably think I'm portraying education as a darkly comedic version of *Survivor*, where teachers cling on by their fingernails, dodging complaints, sidestepping administrative landmines and praying for a miracle. But in reality, for every horror story, every tear-your-hair-out moment, there's a glimmer of light that reminds us why we stay. For every parent who's sent a scathing email at midnight, there's one who's shown up with nothing but appreciation. And for every SLT member who seems more suited to *The Apprentice*, there's another who embodies genuine leadership and grace.

Sure, the job is relentless, but it's also where you'll find some of the best people you could hope to meet. Most teachers are selfless warriors who plug away every day, in unenviable conditions, and still manage to bring light into the lives of young people. And yes, while some students and parents may make you question your sanity, there are others who restore your faith in humanity with a simple "thank you" or a heartfelt gesture. These moments might not grab headlines, but they're powerful reminders of why we're here.

The Parents Who Stand by Us

Let's talk about the parents who see teachers as partners, not as opponents in a courtroom drama. These parents might not write glowing reviews online or launch fan clubs, but they're the steady supporters who make a world of difference. They're the ones who take your side when you telephone them to discuss a concern, who encourage their children to respect your rules, and who remind us that parenting and teaching work best in tandem.

I remember one parent who would always ask, "How can I help support what you're doing in the classroom?" No demands or accusations, just simple, constructive partnership. It generated respect and fostered collaboration to help the child succeed. For every parent who's convinced their child walks on water, there's another who acknowledges that maybe, just maybe, their kid could use a little guidance.

These parents are the gold standard. The ones who make you feel seen, respected and even valued. They're the ones who send thank-you notes at the end of the year or show up at parents' evening with nothing but gratitude. I've met parents who've said things like, "I know you're doing everything you can for them, and I just wanted you to know how much we appreciate it". Those words are worth more than any bottle of wine or box of chocolates that you might be lucky enough to be gifted at Christmastime.

The Students Who Surprise You

Then there are the students. Sure, we've all encountered our fair share of little rebels, but every once in a while, a student reminds you exactly why you signed up for this gig in the first place.

There was one student I had years ago – a quiet, unassuming child who struggled academically but tried his hardest every single day. He might not have been a top performer, but he put his heart into everything he did, and he always said "thank you" after each lesson. Years later, he came back to visit, now a confident young adult, just to say, "Thank you for believing in me when I didn't believe in myself."

Moments like that stick with you. They're the stories we carry in our back pockets, the memories we cling to on the rough days when we wonder if we're making a difference. Because for all the challenging students you encounter, there's one who reminds you that teaching isn't just a job, it's a vocation.

The Colleagues Who Are More Like Family

Let's not forget the wonderful colleagues that you encounter on your educational odyssey. The teachers who carry each other, who lean in to laugh when crying feels too close an option, and who would give their last piece of chocolate to a staff member in need. These are people who may be struggling with their own challenges at work, but still lend a supportive hand, and still walk into the classroom with a smile, ready to give it their all. They don't do it for praise or accolades, they do it because they genuinely care. And it's this spirit, this unrelenting dedication, that turns a school into more than just a workplace.

Teachers are family – a family that understands the highs, the lows and everything in between. They're the ones who calm you when you're on your last nerve, who cover your class when you're overwhelmed and who listen when you need to rant. I've shared so many jokes and moments of triumph with colleagues who have turned into lifelong friends. They're legends in their own right; the people who make you proud to be part of this tribe.

The SLT Members Who Lead by Example

It would be remiss of me not to mention management, or a select few of them at least. Yes, I know I've said a few choice words about some of them, but while there are certainly a number of SLT members who act like they're on a power trip, there are also a precious handful who lead with heart and empathy.

I worked under a headteacher once who was so beloved that, when he retired, the entire school turned out to celebrate him. Staff wore masks with his face on them, and we all gathered to show our appreciation. To anyone who didn't work in or attend the school, the whole event must have seemed over the top, but it was all in good fun – a testament to the love and respect he had earned.

This headteacher led by example; he was always quick to roll up his sleeves and never asked anyone to do something he wouldn't do himself. He knew every teacher well, checked in regularly, and would always ask you how you were. He understood that teachers are human, not just cogs in the educational machine, and that genuine support is a two-way street. When he finally left, there wasn't a dry eye in the school. We lost not just a dedicated headteacher but a true friend, a leader who made us all better just by being there.

And it's not just headteachers. I've had line managers who went above and beyond to advocate for their team, who shouldered the burden when things went wrong and shared the praise when things went right. These are the leaders who make you want to show up for work and be part of a team charged with making the lives of young people better.

The Heroes Behind the Scenes

In every great school, there's a team of unsung heroes. The administrative staff who juggle mountains of paperwork so we don't have to, the teaching assistants who support students one-on-one and the cleaners who transform disaster zones back into classrooms overnight. They might not get the recognition they deserve, but without them, the whole system would crumble.

I once worked with a school secretary who knew every student by name, who could calm a stressed parent (or teacher!) in a flash and who made it her mission to make the school feel like a second home. These people are the heart and soul of every school.

The True Reward

We've all heard it said that teaching is a thankless job, and in many ways, it is. But those "thank you" moments, however few and far between, are the ones that make all the stress worth it. The students who return years later to express gratitude, the parents who write thank-you cards and emails, the grateful hug of a colleague whose class you covered when they needed a break – these are the moments you won't read about in any Ofsted report, but they hold far more weight.

In the end, it's not about the salary, the hours or the endless paperwork. It's about the people – the ones who make this job so meaningful. And those are the unsung heroes we don't always talk about, but we know deep down, are the reason we stay.

CHAPTER 25

MY FINAL WORD

I feel like I'm halfway through my career, but already ageing in dog years. Retirement is a fantasy – one that drifts further away every time someone in Westminster comes up with a new idea about working "a bit longer". I can't see myself making it to 68 in this job without something giving way – physically or mentally.

Every year follows the same script. Come June and July, the sun's shining, students are handing over thank-you cards with awkward smiles, and suddenly the job feels just about bearable. You start deluding yourself: *Maybe it's not so bad.*

Then October rolls in. And with it, the crash. The tiredness hits like a freight train. The motivation drains from your body. You wake up heavy. The dread creeps in. Then it's November and the first resignation list lands in your inbox. Names of staff quietly backing away from the fire.

And again in March. Another list. More good people calling it a day. Some new, some veterans. All of them tired. All of them done — or hoping the next school will be better than the one they're leaving. You glance through the names and you're not even surprised anymore. You just nod.

And that's when it hits you: you're morphing. Slowly. Inevitably. Into one of those teachers you used to look at with a mix of pity and fear. The ones who never smiled. Who looked like they were just surviving, not teaching. I used to think, *God, I'll never end up like that.*

But I have. Or I'm getting there. One timetable change at a time.

If you've made it this far, chances are you're not just reading this book — you've felt it. Like the teachers who shared their stories in these pages, you've seen the cracks in the system and felt them widen beneath your feet.

Maybe you've lived it as a teacher. Or maybe you've watched it slowly consume someone you knew — seen the light fade from their eyes, the weight settle in their shoulders, the spark replaced by spreadsheets and silence.

You've heard the stories: the gaslighting emails, the "urgent" SLT drop-ins, the impossible data drops, the baseless accusations, the tears behind locked classroom doors. The fake smiles. The backstabbing. The Ofsted pantomime. The days where even staying upright felt like a win.

Would I choose teaching again?

Let me answer clearly: not like this. Not in a system that rewards compliance over conscience. Not where survival is praised and questioning is punished. Not when you're expected to bleed out quietly in the name of resilience. Not when integrity gets you labelled "difficult".

I didn't write this book to fix the system — who am I to be that audacious? That ship has long sailed. I wrote it out of frustration.

TEACH, SURVIVE, REPEAT

And maybe, just maybe, to reach the people still oblivious to the truth I only saw clearly ten years in.

I wrote it to hold up a mirror. To show what we've tolerated. What we've normalised. What we've quietly accepted as "just part of the job" for far too long.

And for those determined to stay in the system: teach, survive, repeat.

SPECIAL THANKS

This book wouldn't have been possible without the unfiltered honesty, camaraderie and shared resilience of the online teaching community, particularly the incredible members of Life After Teaching – Exit the Classroom and Thrive. Your stories – raw, funny, heartbreaking and inspiring – formed the backbone of this book. Every post and comment reminded me of the shared struggles we face and the incredible strength it takes to keep going. From tales of burnout to triumphant career changes, your experiences brought depth and authenticity to these pages. For every teacher who felt lost, for every member who hesitated to hit "post", know that your courage in sharing your journey made a difference – not just to me but to countless others searching for solidarity and hope.

REFERENCES

[i] *The Guardian* (2024, December 21) *UK teachers should be allowed to work from home, education secretary says*. Retrieved from https://www.theguardian.com/education/2024/dec/21/uk-teachers-should-be-allowed-to-work-from-home-education-secretary-says.

[ii] Ofqual. (n.d.). *GCSE outcomes: Analytics and reports*. Retrieved January 1 2025, from https://analytics.ofqual.gov.uk/apps/GCSE/Outcomes/

[iii] *The Telegraph*. (2014, July 3) CBI: Too many school leavers underequipped for life. Retrieved from https://www.telegraph.co.uk/education/educationnews/10943278/CBI-too-many-school-leavers-underequipped-for-life.html

[iv] Life After Teaching – Exit the Classroom and Thrive. n.d. Facebook. Accessed Nov 2024. Available at: https://www.facebook.com/groups/LifeAfterTeachingExitTheClassroomAndThrive

[v] BBC News. (2015, March 27). *False allegations can blight teaching, says ATL union*. Retrieved January 1 2025, from https://www.bbc.co.uk/news/education-32078187

[vi] Life After Teaching – Exit the Classroom and Thrive. n.d. Facebook. Accessed Nov 2024. Available at: https://www.facebook.com/groups/LifeAfterTeachingExitTheClassroomAndThrive

[vii] Education Support. (n.d.). Teacher Wellbeing Index. Education Support. Retrieved January 1, 2025, from https://www.educationsupport.org.uk/resources/for-organisations/research/teacher-wellbeing-index/?utm_source=chatgpt.com

[viii] *The Guardian* (2025, March 16) Hundreds of English academy heads paid over £150k, as number on 'gravy train' doubles in five *years*. Available at https://www.theguardian.com/education/2025/mar/16/hundreds-of-english-academy-heads-paid-over-150k-as-number-on-gravy-train-doubles-in-five-years

[ix] *The Guardian*. (2021, April 6). *"Very intimidating": Teachers on sexual harassment by pupils*. Retrieved from https://www.theguardian.com/education/2021/apr/06/very-intimidating-teachers-on-sexual-harassment-by-pupils

[x] Life After Teaching – Exit the Classroom and Thrive. n.d. Facebook. Accessed Nov 2024. Available at: https://www.facebook.com/groups/LifeAfterTeachingExitTheClassroomAndThrive

[xi] National Education Union. (n.d.). *It's Just Everywhere: Sexual Harassment in UK Schools*. Retrieved from https://neu.org.uk/latest/library/its-just-everywhere

[xii] Legislation.gov.uk. (2010). *Equality Act 2010, Section 26: Harassment*. Retrieved from https://www.legislation.gov.uk/ukpga/2010/15/section/26

[xiii] Education Support. (2020). *Teacher Wellbeing Index 2020*. Retrieved from https://teachershub.educationsupport.org.uk/sites/default/files/2021-03/Teacher%20Wellbeing%20Index%202020.pdf?utm_source=chatgpt.com

Printed in Dunstable, United Kingdom